"GRAND FASHIONABLE N[IGHTS] KENDAL THEATRE 1575-1985

by

Margaret Eddershaw

Centre for North-West Regional Studies
University of Lancaster
Occasional Paper No. 17

1989

General Editor: Oliver M. Westall

ISSN 0308-4310
ISBN 0-901-272-62-0

We should like to acknowledge the generous support of the Francis C. Scott Charitable Trust for this publication.

This volume is the seventeenth in a series of occasional papers in which contributions to the study of the North West are published by the Centre for North West Regional Studies in the University of Lancaster and are available from there. The general editor will be pleased to consider manuscripts of between 10,000 and 25,000 words on topics in the natural or social sciences and humanities which relate to the counties of Lancashire or Cumbria.

PREVIOUS TITLES

Printed in England by Titus Wilson & Son Ltd., Kendal, Cumbria

CONTENTS

ILLUSTRATIONS

Preface

Cultural history is usually seen in terms of artists operating in a limited number of centres of excellence. This history of the theatre in Kendal penetrates behind this glossy façade. It shows how the lives of men and women in a more modest provincial centre were enriched by the excitement, magic and mystery of the stage.

Margaret Eddershaw shows us the changing nature of the entertainment offered, but her account is of far wider interest. She places theatre within the context of local society: its structure, attitudes and economic circumstances. It has never evolved in a vacuum. Its possibilities are created by the view of life taken by its patrons and the business considerations which govern its provision. This is clearly demonstrated here. The theatre in Kendal evolved originally from a local religious impulse. In the eighteenth century, served by touring companies, it became a focal point in the life of a thriving county society and an apparently successful business enterprise. In the nineteenth century its vigour was constrained by moral earnestness and a fear of loss of social control when people enjoyed themselves. In the twentieth century, technological change created the cinema, but new patronage was found from the business community to support a remarkable revival in local live theatre.

In short, a history of the theatre in Kendal would in itself be important, but this is more. It is a fresh new perspective on the whole history of the town. In this, it helps us to understand better the provincial life which most Englishmen have shared.

Oliver M. Westall

Introduction

In many ways Kendal has been a provincial town that in its general dramatic tastes and trends has reflected or followed those of the country as a whole during a period of about 400 years. Kendal, in common with many towns, had its own cycle of mystery plays; built a new playhouse in the 1750s (like Norwich, Bath); and another later in the century (like Richmond, Lancaster). Around 1800, theatre in Kendal, as elsewhere, flourished: what London saw in one year, Kendal had seen by the next; if the metropolis loved comic opera and then melodrama, Kendal soon followed suit. When theatre declined in other towns and cities in the 1830s, so it did in Kendal. In the mid nineteenth century, Kendal, like most places, saw a broad variety of entertainment; its interest in theatre was then revived by the national touring companies, taking the cultural life of the town into the twentieth century, when theatre met the competition of the new media of film and television. In all that, Kendal appears to be a typical provincial town.

But beneath the surface, other factors made Kendal less typical. The special social structure of nineteenth century Kendal, in particular the control of the town by a powerful group of non-conformist industrialists in the first part of the century, led to an unusual amount of overt opposition to some leisure pursuits, and especially to theatre. Reflected in the struggles for social and political power in the town; in the conflict between the old established Anglican/Tory attitudes to "culture" and the Quaker/Liberal values of hard work and abstemiousness, theatre lost out.

Part of the non-conformist influence over social values and attitudes resulted from Kendal's isolation and from its self-sufficiency. The sense of independence and of a very individual identity in the town has not faded during the intervening years. Kendal today, although part of a large and flourishing tourist industry, has retained the atmosphere of a closely-knit community, and it is possible to see the effect of this on the contemporary theatre in the town.

Acknowledgements

I am grateful to Miss Sybil Rosenfeld for permitting me to use her notes on Kendal Playbills and to quote from her unpublished paper, "History of the Georgian Theatre, Richmond, Yorkshire, and its Circuit" (1960); to the staff of the Westmorland Record Office and Kendal Public Library (Local Collection) for their invaluable assistance; and to Keith Sturgess, the supervisor of my original thesis on which this account is based.

I should like to thank Arthur Thompson for the photographs and also the Westmorland Gazette, Associated Book Publishers and the Theatre Collection, University of Bristol for permission to reproduce Fig. 11 and the cover plate respectively.

Margaret Eddershaw

Notes
The following abbreviated references will be used in all the notes:
W.R.O.   Westmorland Record Office.
C.N.   C. Nicholson, *The Annals of Kendal*, 2nd ed., 1961.
J.F.C.   J. F. Curwen, *Kirbie-Kendall*, Kendal 1900
W.G.   *Westmorland Gazette and Kendal Advertizer.*
K.C.   *Kendal Advertizer and Kendal Chronicle.*
S.R.I.   S. Rosenfeld, "The XVIII Century Theatre at Richmond", York Georgian Society, 1947.
S.R.II   S. Rosenfeld, "History of the Georgian Theatre at Richmond, Yorkshire and Its Circuit", 1960 (unpublished paper).
S.R.III S. Rosenfeld's notes on Kendal playbills.

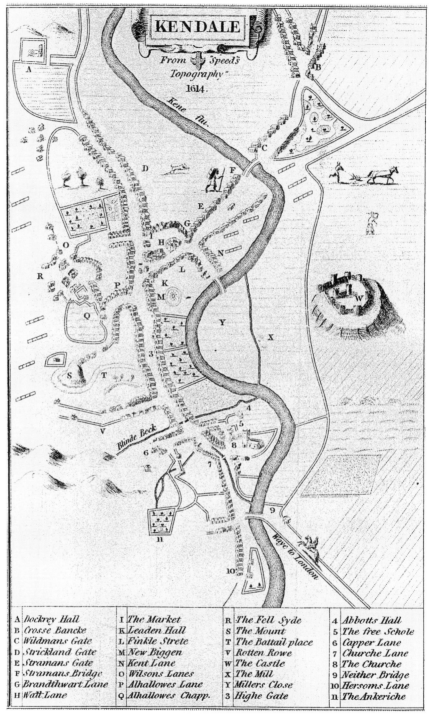

A	Dockrey Hall	I	The Market	R	The Fell Syde	4	Abbotts Hall
B	Crosse Bancke	K	Leaden Hall	S	The Mount	5	The free Schole
C	Wildmans Gate	L	Finkle Strete	T	The Battail place	6	Capper Lane
D	Strickland Gate	M	New Biggen	V	Rotten Rowe	7	Churche Lane
E	Stramans Gate	N	Kent Lane	W	The Castle	8	The Churche
F	Stramans Bridge	O	Wilsons Lanes	X	The Mill	9	Neither Bridge
G	Brandthwart Lane	P	Alhallowes Lane	Y	Millers Close	10	Hersoms Lane
H	Wall Lane	Q	Alhallowes Chapp.	3	Highe Gate	11	The Ankeriche

Fig. 1   Speed's map of Kendal, 1614
(from C. Nicholson, *Annals of Kendal*, 1861)

Prologue
"To these Minstrels enteres a Sot": Theatrical Activity in Kendal 1575-1750

In 1671, Kendal was described by Sir Daniel Fleming in his *History of Westmorland:*

> Kendall, or rather Kirby Kendale (writ antiently Kirby in Kendale, that is the church town in Kendale). It is the chief town for largeness, neatness, buildings and trade in this country, and is most pleasantly seated, on the most part, on the west bank of the river Kent . . . It hath two broad and long streets, fairly built, crossing the one over the other, two large stone bridges, and one of wood. It hath also a fair church . . .[1]

The chief trade of this pleasant town then was the manufacturing of a coarse woollen cloth called "Kendal green". Kendal had been established as a centre for the woollen trade in the early fourteenth century and on the strength of this prospered for several centuries with little competition, indeed, "Kendal green" became a household name. For example, Falstaff, in *Henry IV, Part I*, claims that he was attacked by "Three misbegotten knaves in Kendal green".[2]

The Charter of 1575 that made Kendal a borough also established two annual fairs, which, no doubt, attracted a number of travelling entertainers. Ballads and northern jigs were typical entertainment of the Westmorland and Cumberland region and it

> was also the home and natural setting for many legends of Arthur, which in the late fifteenth and early sixteenth century became attached to the country round Penrith, maintaining the supremacy of the traditional British hero like Harry Hotspur. Here the traditional form of entertainer, like the minstrel, lingered longest.[3]

Of course, the townsfolk of Kendal did not just wait for these travelling players to arrive, but created their own entertainment as well. During Passion Week, for example, Kendal youths, dressed as minstrels, sang songs about "pace-egging" and performed a "mummer's" play. This play continued to be performed well into the nineteenth century and an account of it is given in *The Lonsdale Magazine* of 1821:

> To these minstrels enteres a Sot dressed in a motley dress, with a mask on his face, imitating a carbuncled face. He has a bell to his Cap, which tinkles as he staggers round the circle after the sailor. He also has a piece of tin and silk in his mouth, such as is used for Punch in a puppet show; and when he tries to sing he can make nothing but a squeak . . .[4]

This is, of course, a local version of the mumming traditional throughout the country.

Kendal's craftsmen were also involved (in the fifteenth and sixteenth centuries) in presenting mystery plays. Indeed, it seems that Kendal saw some of the last performances of such pieces. The well-known, extant cycles of Wakefield and Coventry ceased to be performed in 1576 and 1579, respectively, yet Kendal's

1

Corporation Minutes for September 1586 show that local opinion was in favour of the revival of mystery play performances in the town:

FFOR THE PLAYE

Forasmuch as Very many and dyvers of the Common Inhabitants of this Incorporacun . . . do covytt and earnestlye Crye for the havinge of Corpus Xti play yearlye usuallye to be had played and used heare as in former tyme . . .[5]

It seems that performances of the *Corpus Christi* play were then revived and that they actually continued into the next century. John Weever, a native of Lancashire, gives a first hand account in his *Ancient Funerall Monuments* (1631):

They call this Corpus Christi play in my countrey, which I have seen acted at Preston, and Lancaster, and last of all at Kendall, in the beginning of the raigne of King James: for which the Townesmen were sore troubled; and upon good reasons the play finally supprest, not only there, but in all the other towns of the Kingdome.[6]

But the custom of playing this pageant may have survived even longer: Thomas Heywood, the playwright, in his *An Apology for Actors*, published in 1612, claimed:

To this day in divers places of England there be townes that hold the priviledge of their faires, and other characters by yearely stage-plays, as at Manningtree in Suffolke, Kendall in the north and others.

The fact that Kendal did not appear to hold its Charter on any such condition may cast doubt upon the whole statement, but in any case, it does seem to have been one of the last towns in which mystery plays were performed.

However, it is another century before we get the first extant reference to a *professional* performance of a play in Kendal. This comes in the manuscript "Memoranda" of Benjamin Browne of Troutbeck, who was Kendal's High Constable from 1711 till 1732. His memoranda are for the most part daily financial accounts, and are, therefore, tantalisingly brief. On November 30, 1722, Browne notes in his record of a visit to Kendal: "My ffamily gooing to a play 1 = 0". And in November 1727, Browne spent 4-6½d in "Kendall at play-house". The amount, which is surprisingly high, may well have included other expenses, and the mention of a "playhouse" need not necessarily imply the performance was in a custom-built theatre; a room in an inn was as likely a venue. Browne visited the theatre again in 1729, twice in one week:

April 19. Kendall. At playhouse 1 = 6
April 24. Kendall. Two tickets for ye playhouse 3 = 0[8]

He does not record any further visits in his memoranda, though his grandson, also called Benjamin, continued the family tradition both by becoming High Constable and by going to the theatre (see Act I).

Evidence of other early eighteenth century performances in Kendal is supplied by the town's first newspaper, the *Kendal Weekly Courant*. In the first year of its publication (1731/2) it carried several accounts of and advertisements for entertainments in the town. On March 4 it reported that "a very splendid Entertainment" had been given at the White Lyon by a Mr. Robert Cecil; and in May, "A Consort of Vocal and Instrumental Musick, by four voices from

2

London" was announced.[9] The following month the news was given of another forthcoming attraction from London:

> We have an account from Penreth [sic], that there is a Company of Comedians from London now there, and they will stay during the time of the Races and that they intend to be in this Town in a month's time.[10]

The company was evidently timing the visit to coincide with Kendal races, which were usually held in July and August, in the expectation of a ready audience. On July 25, 1731/2, the newspaper announced the performance of "the Wriggling of the merry Thought, a new & entertaining Diversion", presumably presented by this company, and it seems they were still in Kendal on August 19:

> We hear that on Monday next, for the Benefit of Mr. and Mrs. Emett, will be a Tragedy call'd The London Merchant, or The History of George Barnwell. With the Comical Tragedy of Tom Thumb.[11]

So Kendal was being given the opportunity to see the very latest in metropolitan entertainment: Fielding's *Tom Thumb* was first presented in London in April 1730, while *The London Merchant* had only received its first performance in June 1731. Unfortunately the newspapers do not tell us how Kendal received these events nor do they give any more news of theatre in the town during the first half of the eighteenth century. The next important recorded "theatrical" date is that of the town's first identifiable playhouse.

Notes
  1. Quoted by N. Nicholson, *The Lake District: An Anthology*, 1977, p. 224.
  2. Act II, scene iv.
  3. M. Bradbrook, *The Rise of the Common Player*, 1962, p. 22.
  4. J. Briggs, ed., *The Lonsdale Magazine, II,*, Kirkby Lonsdale, 1821.
  5. R. S. Ferguson, ed., *The Boke of Recorde of Kirbie Kendall*, 1892, p. 136.
  6. p. 405.
  7. p. 61.
  8. In W.R.O.
  9. *Kendal Weekly Courant*, June 17, 1732.
  10. *Ibid*. August 19, 1732.

Act I:
"Grand Fashionable Nights": Kendal Theatre
Flourishes (1758-1817)

The first clearly recorded playhouse in Kendal was situated in the north-east corner of the Market Place. The original property dates from the seventeenth century; surprisingly the building still stands. It is, however, difficult to glean much about the theatre from its present condition as it has inevitably undergone considerable alteration in the past three hundred years. The theatre was a conversion of a building in a small group of houses and shops, which had been bought in 1636 on behalf of the corporation by Thomas Sleddal, Kendal's first mayor. Over two of the shops was a large weigh-loft that was subsequently used for a hundred years for weighing wool. In 1758 the shops and weigh-loft were bought by Thomas Ashburner, a Kendal printer and bookseller, who converted the loft into a theatre. The Conveyance of May 20, 1758, describes it as:

> One large Room or Apartment . . . lately erected and built by the said Thomas Ashburner
> . . . and now commonly called and known by the Name of The New Theatre or the
> Playhouse.[1]

Whether the name "New Theatre" indicates that this was not the first playhouse is impossible to discover, but it is suggested by the local historian, Cornelius Nicholson, that the theatre comprised more than the area of the weigh-loft. His account reads:

> The first theatre that we can make out with certainty, was a building in the Market Place,
> approached by a flight of steps, which led to the dwelling over part of the Foot Ball Inn and
> the adjoining premises.[2]

The Foot Ball Inn (which no longer exists) adjoined the theatre building on the west side and until the end of the nineteenth century showed signs of the gallery front, an architectural feature very common in Kendal. The original stone steps still lead into the first floor room which is thought to have been the theatre. The room itself is relatively small for a theatre: 10.5 metres long and 6 metres wide. There is no evidence now to suggest that the room extended into the building next door, the old Foot Ball Inn. The ceiling height is – and was – only 2.75 metres, for, although there is a second floor, the beams between the two are original. The present windows in the room were put in during the nineteenth century, as was one of the fireplaces in the east wall. The other may be earlier. It is possible that the large barn north-east of the room provided dressing room space, as the wall between the two is less substantial than the others. (See Fig. 2.) The height of the room would only permit one gallery, so the theatre probably held between 120 and 150 people. This, Kendal's first playhouse, was very simple, similar, in fact, to the large rooms available in many inns of the town.

We do not know what prompted Thomas Ashburner to build a theatre, though

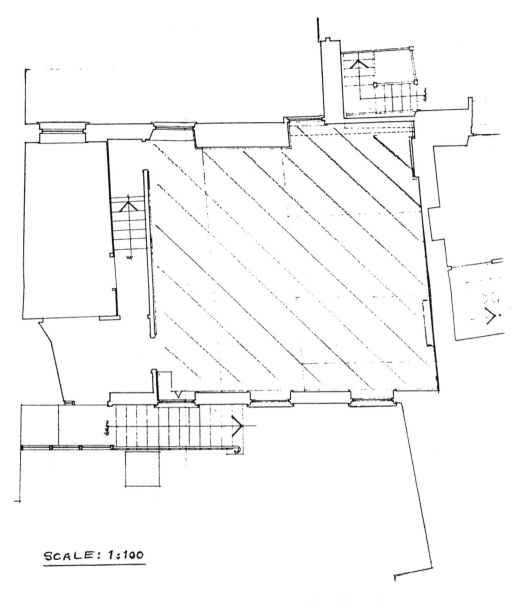

SCALE: 1:100

Fig. 2   Ground plan of 'Market Place Theatre'
(from plans made by South Lakeland District Council in 1978)

he was an important local businessman who had some literary interests, being editor of the *Kendal Weekly Courant* and the *Kendal Weekly Mercury*. Also, he was evidently anxious to encourage other arts; he was one of two witnesses who signed the Indenture that made George Romney apprentice to a Kendal artist in 1755.[3]

Nothing is known of the first actors who performed in this playhouse. No playbills have survived from that period and none of the extant local or regional newspapers mentions the Kendal theatre until the 1790s. The earliest reference to actors in Kendal during the second half of the eighteenth century is made by the actor, Thomas Holcroft, in his autobiography. Holcroft, son of a Lancashire shoemaker, performed at Kendal in 1774. He gives a brief, but telling, description of John Stanton, the manager, with whose company he performed, and of the company itself:

> Our manager has five sons and daughters all ranked as performers; so that he sweeps eleven shares, that is, nearly half the profits of the theatre, into his pocket every night . . . They have a circuit or set of towns, to which they resort when the time comes round; so that there are but three or four in our company who are not well known in Kendal.[4]

In the provinces in the eighteenth century there were three types of companies: the circuit companies, who toured an established number of towns, taking up residence in each for a few months at a time; the innumerable troupes of "strollers", who performed at any town or village that would permit them and lived very much from hand to mouth; and the temporary companies from London, that undertook provincial tours during the summer when the metropolitan theatres were closed. The Act of 1737 (usually known as the "Vagrant Act") had made acting illegal in the provinces, though many companies ignored the law and lived with their "rogues and vagabond" reputation. Others managed to obtain permission for performances from local magistrates; or the latter turned a "blind-eye" unless a local inhabitant complained; or the law was evaded by presenting the play *gratis* between two parts of a concert. In 1788 an act was passed legalising acting in the provinces by endowing local magistrates with the power to licence a company for sixty days at a stretch, provided their visit was not repeated within eight months. This act, which was really meant to control more tightly the vast numbers of provincial players, ironically greatly stimulated theatrical growth in the provinces, and the circuit companies became firmly established.

These companies usually timed their visits to coincide with local fairs or assizes which created an influx into the town from surrounding areas, an atmosphere of public holiday, and thus a potentially large audience. The usual number of actors in such companies was about twenty and they were organized and controlled by an actor-manager. As Thomas Holcroft explained, the traditional financial system in the early companies was "sharing", and the actors relied a great deal on their "benefits". Each member of the company would have a benefit performance, or share one with another actor, in each town of the circuit, and for these the actor had to sell his own tickets by calling on local patrons and trying to persuade them to attend.

6

Quite early in the eighteenth century, provincial companies instituted benefits for local charities, as a way of securing the goodwill of the town, and one expression of reciprocal goodwill was the "bespoke" performance, for which a local individual or body chose a play and either bought a large number of tickets to distribute or paid a subsidy. These performances were usually advertised as a "Grand Fashionable Night".

Among the many hardships of life in a circuit company was, of course, the travelling, which was both difficult and expensive. Many actors were forced to walk from one theatre to the next, in some instances carrying not only their belongings but also the scenery and costumes. F. C. Wemyss, an actor who was in the company that performed in Kendal in 1815, describes in his autobiography the company's journey to Northallerton, the next town on their circuit:

> We allowed ourselves two days to accomplish the task, walking twenty miles before breakfast the first day, fourteen to dinner, and fourteen after dinner; thus accomplishing forty eight miles the first day, over mountainous country, and leisurely walking fifteen miles the following day.[5]

The date when Kendal's first known theatre went out of theatrical use is the subject of much debate among the local historians of the nineteenth century (there are none earlier). W. Sayer claims that in about 1773 drama was so popular that another larger theatre was built elsewhere in the town;[6] Nicholson gives the year as 1777 "when the histrionic art was encouraged in Kendal, that building [Market Place theatre] was deemed inconveniently small".[7] This is a likely date for some kind of change, since Thomas Ashburner died in 1778 leaving his property to his son, James.[8] Nicholson also claims that the congregation of the Independent Chapel met in this "old theatre" until their new chapel was built.[9] That would mean they occupied the theatre sometime between 1772 and 1782, whereas John Curwen asserts that this sect met elsewhere during that period. To complicate the matter even further, on a map dated 1787, and based on a survey by John Todd, the theatre is still marked in its Market Place position. (See Fig. 3.) Most of the historians agree, however, that the theatre was rented by the Methodists in the autumn of 1787, so by then at least, it was almost certainly no longer a playhouse. And the rest of the building's history is swiftly told. In February 1795, "the Burgagehouse called the Old Theatre" was sold to Elizabeth Prickett, a widow, by the trustees of the will of James Ashburner.[10] The building was used as shops until 1843, when it was made into a Workmen's Newsroom. In 1877 it became the Working Men's Institute,[11] the notice for which is still on the front of the building, though it now houses an estate agent's business. (See Fig. 4.)

It is suggested by Henry Duncan in his *Reminiscences of Persons and Places in Kendal Sixty Years Ago* (1890) that after the Market Place theatre closed, a room in a building known as "The Fold" in Stricklandgate was used for performances. This building was pulled down before the end of the nineteenth century, but Curwen describes it as an "old lath and plaster house", and asserts that it had a room, large enough to hold 300 people, which was at one time used

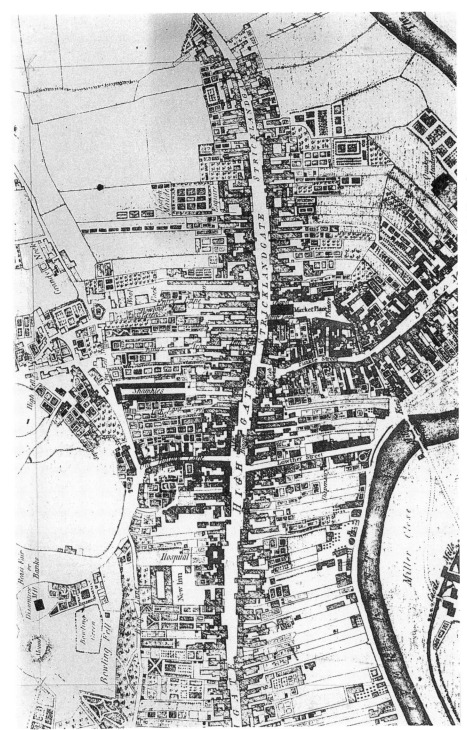

Fig. 3 Todd's map of Kendal, 1787 (from original in Kendal Public Library)

8

Fig. 4 Exterior of the Market Place theatre building, 1988

in this way, and Nicholson claims that theatre business moved directly from the Market Place to the Woolpack Yard in 1777.[13]

In moving on to examine the history of Kendal's second recorded playhouse (in Woolpack Yard) we are again confronted by conflicting opinions from the historians. Curwen gives the opening date of the new theatre as 1789, whereas Sybil Rosenfeld claims that there were, in fact, *TWO* theatres in Woolpack Yard, one built in the 1770s, a second in 1789 or 1790. She writes:

> Mr. R. M. Brock has pointed out that the first Woolpack Yard playhouse was built in 1776/7. He says that this date is confirmed by the deeds which he has seen.[14]

It has not been possible to locate these deeds, but further support for this early date for the theatre may come from the unpublished manuscript parts of James Winston's *The Theatric Tourist* (1805), which gives brief details of a large number of eighteenth century provincial playhouses. The Kendal entry reads:

Kendal – Butler
    Feb. 1797
    About 1778
                                     Butler Minor
                                         Austin
                                       Collins[15]

These cryptic notes are very interesting. Butler was the manager of the Kendal theatre (whichever building it was) from 1785 till 1811, and his company was certainly in the town on February 1797. The second date in Winston's notes could, therefore, be a building date.

One possible answer to the conflicting dates is that the theatre of the 1770s was demolished in order to make space for the second one of 1789/90. The first building was bought in 1786 by Thomas Fenton, who also owned the Woolpack Inn (in the same yard). The deeds of the inn contain an abstract (1794) that seems to support the notion that the "theatre" building was already a playhouse when Fenton made the purchase:

> And also all those several burgage buildings dwellinghouses warehouses and Theatre with the garden thereunto belonging situate standing lying and being in or near the sd. Wool Pack Yard . . . then formerly purchased by the sd. Thos. Fenton . . .[16]

The abstract indicates that the theatre had a garden, and later passages show that it also had its own yard, but there would have been no place for a garden and yard adjacent to the "second" theatre, which is extant. Presumably, the document is, therefore, referring to an earlier theatre. If the second one was indeed built on the same land, this would also account for the space shown where it now stands on the map of 1787 (Fig. 3).

It was said that the (second) Woolpack Yard playhouse was "a neat building, regularly built",[17] and more specifically that it was "on the plan of the metropolitan theatres".[18] Allowing for provincial exaggeration, this building could fit that description; its pleasing Georgian proportions are still conspicuous. It is 23 metres long, 10.75 metres wide and approximately 9 metres high internally. Also there is a good 2 metres high cellar beneath most of the "ground" floor (which is itself raised above the yard level by about 1 metre). This cellar could have provided space for stage-machinery, traps, dressing-rooms and even a sunken pit, though there is no evidence for any of these now. (See Fig. 5.) Kendal's Woolpack Yard Theatre was, in fact, larger than the well-known Georgian Theatre at Richmond (Yorkshire), which provides an interesting comparison with several of Kendal's playhouses, particularly because at one time the two towns were part of the same circuit.

The Richmond theatre was built in 1788 and is a slightly irregular building, 18.75 metres long and 8.75 metres wide. The stage has two proscenium doors, above which are stage-boxes. (See Fig. 6.) The Woolpack Yard Theatre also had boxes; an entry in a diary written by an unnamed young lady of Kendal describes seeing a play from the "Stage-Box" in February 1795.[19] The decor of this theatre seems to have been elegant; the boxes and pit were lined, probably with some attractive silk, and the house was obviously well maintained, since there are a number of references to its redecoration in later years.

F. C. Wemyss, who acted in this theatre in 1815, described it as being "capable of holding from sixty to seventy pounds".[20] It was usual in that period to estimate the size of a theatre by the amount that could be taken in one night at the box-office; Wemyss' estimate implies that the Woolpack Yard could have held between 600 and 700 people. The earliest information on a company in this theatre comes from a playbill of April 4, 1783, which advertises three plays to be presented *gratis* between the parts of a concert – to evade the law. The

10

Fig. 5   Woolpack Yard theatre building, 1988

company is unnamed but as the announcement is for a benefit performance, they were presumably in Kendal for a season of some kind. Apart from the names of the cast little else can be gleaned about the occasion or the performers.

The next extant playbill for the Kendal theatre – for January 21, 1785 – reveals that a completely different company has taken over, and this date marks the beginning of a long period of stability in the town's theatre history, when it became part of a Richmond company's circuit. It is thus possible to trace the fortunes of Kendal's theatre by means of a detailed examination of the activities of this company. (See Fig. 7.)

The manager of this Richmond company in the very early 1770's had been a Mr. Wright, who became the second husband of a Mrs. Tryphosa Miller. When Wright died, his wife, in addition to acting, took over the company management for a while. But by 1773 she had married an actor, Samuel Butler, and he, her third husband, became manager; he was twenty-three and his wife was forty-six. The company included in their circuit at this time Guisborough and Harrogate.

11

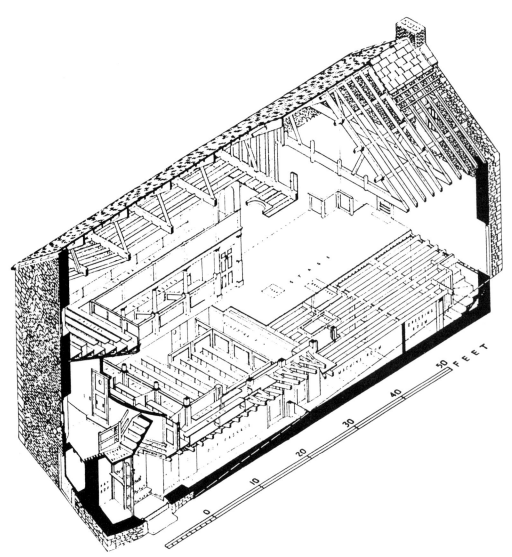

Fig. 6   Scale reconstruction of Georgian Theatre, Richmond
(from *The Development of the English Playhouse* by Richard Leacroft, by kind permission of
Methuen, London)

That first playbill (of January 21) announces the presentation in Kendal of a
piece by O'Keeffe:

> Mr. Butler flatters himself that the great Applause this piece has received from the most
> brilliant and crowded Audiences in London, will be sufficient to recommend it to the Ladies
> and Gentlemen of Kendal, and afford him some Recompense for the great Expence and
> Trouble he has been at in procuring an Authentic Manuscript copy and the Author's
> Permission to perform it.

12

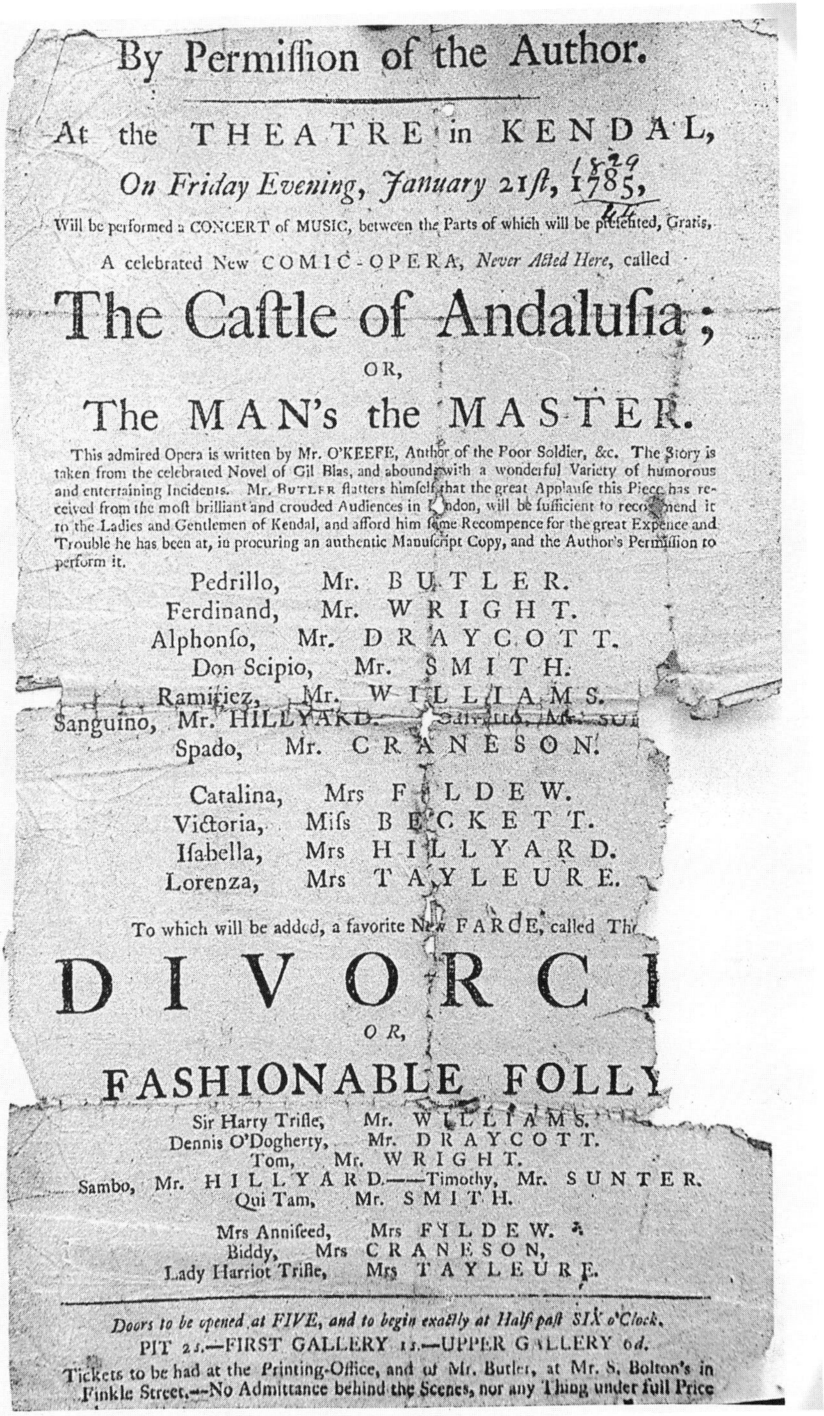

By Permiſſion of the Author.

At the THEATRE in KENDAL,

On Friday Evening, January 21ſt, 1785,

(handwritten: 1829)

Will be performed a CONCERT of MUSIC, between the Parts of which will be preſented, Gratis,

A celebrated New COMIC-OPERA, *Never Acted Here*, called

The Caſtle of Andaluſia;

OR,

The MAN's the MASTER.

This admired Opera is written by Mr. O'KEEFE, Author of the Poor Soldier, &c. The Story is taken from the celebrated Novel of Gil Blas, and abounds with a wonderful Variety of humorous and entertaining Incidents. Mr. BUTLER flatters himſelf that the great Applauſe this Piece has received from the moſt brilliant and crouded Audiences in London, will be ſufficient to recommend it to the Ladies and Gentlemen of Kendal, and afford him ſome Recompence for the great Expence and Trouble he has been at, in procuring an authentic Manuſcript Copy, and the Author's Permiſſion to perform it.

Pedrillo,	Mr.	B U T L E R.
Ferdinand,	Mr.	W R I G H T.
Alphonſo,	Mr.	D R A Y C O T T.
Don Scipio,	Mr.	S M I T H.
Ramirez,	Mr.	W I L L I A M S.
Sanguino,	Mr. HILLYARD.	Saritio, Mr. Sui
Spado,	Mr.	C R A N E S O N.
Catalina,	Mrs	F I L D E W.
Victoria,	Miſs	B E C K E T T.
Iſabella,	Mrs	H I L L Y A R D.
Lorenza,	Mrs	T A Y L E U R E.

To which will be added, a favorite New FARCE, called The

D I V O R C E

OR,

FASHIONABLE FOLLY

Sir Harry Triſle,	Mr.	W I L L I A M S.
Dennis O'Dogherty,	Mr.	D R A Y C O T T.
Tom,	Mr.	W R I G H T.
Sambo, Mr. H I L L Y A R D.——Timothy, Mr. S U N T E R.		
Qui Tam,	Mr.	S M I T H.
Mrs Anniſeed,	Mrs	F I L D E W.
Biddy,	Mrs	C R A N E S O N,
Lady Harriot Triſle,	Mrs	T A Y L E U R E.

Doors to be opened at FIVE, and to begin exactly at Half paſt SIX o'Clock.
PIT 2s.—FIRST GALLERY 1s.—UPPER GALLERY 6d.
Tickets to be had at the Printing-Office, and of Mr. Butler, at Mr. S. Bolton's in Finkle Street.—No Admittance behind the Scenes, nor any Thing under full Price

Fig. 7 Playbill, 1785

The claim of possessing a manuscript copy was a frequent one on the playbills of this period, a time when plays were often slow coming into print, and plagiarism and imitation were rife. But such a statement is testimony to the care and attention Butler gave to his management. His talents, in fact, resided more in management than in acting it seems:

> As an actor he is useful but he has little claim to merit, if we except his Clodpole [in *Barnably Brittle*] . . .
> He fancies he excells in *Scotch* parts, but it is *Yorkshire* he speaks not the Scottish dialect.[21]

There is no evidence of performances in Kendal by the Butler company, nor any other, during the next five years, though Butler continued to visit regularly the other towns in his circuit. Then a playbill, dated 7 February, 1791, announces a performance by Butler's company in Kendal's "New Theatre" in Woolpack Yard. Since the evening's entertainment (which included Butler in his famous part in *Barnaby Brittle*) was openly advertised, and no longer *gratis* between the parts of a concert, it seems the company was now licensed according to the Act of 1788. They were presumably still in Kendal on February 25, when the local High Constable, Benjamin Browne, the younger, spent "2s. 6d." on "play and Exp(enses) at Kendal this night".[22] Browne's subsequent visits to the theatre indicate that the company was also in the town on November 15, 1792, and May 8, 1793. And they had returned to Kendal by December 1794. We have one playbill for this season, dated December 1, but for further details we must rely on the diary of the "unnamed young lady" mentioned earlier. She visited the theatre four times in the spring of 1795, the last time on March 23, when she writes: "Saw Mr. Montague in the Foundlings".

In September 1797, Mrs. Butler died at the age of seventy; she is described in the Richmond Parish Registers as "Tryphosa wife of Samuel Butler comedian". Butler did not remain "unattached" for long. By July 1800 he had married Miss Jefferson, an actress who had joined his company in 1797 and was the daughter of Thomas Jefferson, a well-known actor and manager.

The now customary biennial visit by the Butler Company to Kendal in 1798/9 commenced in November, but we only hear of them at the time of their departure at the end of the season. The *Cumberland Pacquet* for March 12, 1799, announces:

> Mr. Butler's company of comedians left Kendal last week, after performing there generally to full houses, since November last.

For the 1800/1 season, the company included one of the second Mrs. Butler's brothers, George Jefferson, and her sister, Elizabeth. (Another brother, Joseph Jefferson, emigrated and founded the famous Jefferson theatre family in the U.S.A.). Two members of the youngest of the three generations in the company were brought forward during this season. On January 30, Drinkwater Meadows, the son of one of Butler's leading actors, Tom Meadows, appeared (at the age of two or three) as Lady Macduff's son in *Macbeth*; and on February 25, Miss Wright, grand-daughter of the late Tryphosa Butler, performed in *Richard III* as one of the young princes. A significant addition to the repertoire this season

14

was Kendal's first taste of melodrama in the form of Lewis' *The Castle Spectre*, offered "positively for one night only" and with the manager's assurance that no expense had been spared "to render the piece worthy of Kendal's Approbation and Support".[23]

Evidence for Kendal's theatrical activities in the seasons of 1803 and 1805 is sparse but we have a complete set of playbills for 1807. The first important change in that season was that the theatre was called "Theatre Royal", though there is no record of it having been granted royal letters patent. Maybe Butler wished to elevate the theatre's status for its visiting star, announced for January 14: "Mr. Kemble, brother of John Phillip". Stephen Kemble must have been quite an attraction for Kendal in 1807. During his few nights in the town he appeared twice as Falstaff, a part which he is said to have performed at Drury Lane in 1802 without the "stuffing".[24] Although originally only engaged for two nights, he stayed for one extra performance.

The next theatre season in Kendal for which we have firm evidence is that of 1811, which proved to be Samuel Butler's last. He died in June 1812 at Beverley, aged sixty-two. A marble tablet in St. Mary's Church there reads:

> In memory of Samuel Butler, a poor player
> That struts and frets his hour upon the Stage
> And then is heard no more.

His widow took over the management of the company and continued to run it until 1818 (by which time the Kendal theatre had been taken over by another company).

The season of 1813 in Kendal opened on February 1, after Mrs. Butler's company had made a successful visit to Ulverston. The reviewer of the early offerings commented:

> Mrs. Butler's company of comedians, at present in this town, is much improved since they were here two years ago, and . . . the new pieces already performed have been got up with great judgment.[25]

It seems a change of management had been good for the company, and certainly the new manager was greatly appreciated by the Kendal audience. The approval of Mrs. Butler continued when the company returned in 1815 and extended to include her young daughter:

> This company, in its female department has been greatly improved by the addition of Mrs. Butler and her daughter . . . She (Mrs. Butler) is a most estimable woman, off the stage as well as on it and her daughter is a perfect pretty little witch.[26]

Although the Kendal season of 1817 began later than usual (in March) and it was announced that it would only last two instead of the usual three months, the company was offering a very strong attraction in the person of Mrs. Renaud, better known as Mrs. Powell, of the Covent Garden Theatre. F. C. Wemyss writes of Mrs. Renaud:

> Her acting spoke more to the heart than that of any lady I ever saw before or since, identifying herself with the character she was performing, until you forgot the woman in the actress.[27]

Mrs. Renaud had been engaged for four nights. She duly took her Kendal benefit on March 22 but was then re-engaged to play Volumnia in *Coriolanus* and Queen Elizabeth in *The Earl of Essex*. Wemyss' opinion of this actress was apparently shared for she was still with the company in June when she took a second benefit. And although that performance was advertised as her last, she consented to appear as Julia in *The Rivals* for Mrs. Jefferson's benefit on June 17. With the help of Mrs. Renaud the company extended their season in Kendal until July 7. This extra-long stay of four months was to prove a swansong; the company never returned to the town.

The final exit of the Butler company from Kendal's playhouse in 1817 marks a turn in the theatrical fortunes in the town. Local support for the theatre until this point had in general been very strong. In order to understand this evident popularity we should look more closely at the composition of the local audience.

The population of Kendal in the late eighteenth century was about 8,500, and even if we include the outlying rural districts and other nearby Westmorland towns, the potential audience was not large. Also those travelling to the Kendal theatre from outside the town during this period would have needed their own carriages and would, therefore, have been gentry; and Westmorland was among the least "gentrified" counties in England at this time, with only a thin scattering of large estates or socially important families.[28]

As for the class composition of Kendal itself, at the end of the eighteenth century, it was said to have several times fewer gentry *per capita* than the towns of Ambleside, Appleby and Brough. But it did have a good share of well-to-do tradesmen, even in the 1700s, thanks to the wool trade. One important difference between Kendal and most other provincial towns which supported a theatre in the eighteenth and nineteenth centuries was that it did not have County Assizes or Races for most of the period, events on which many circuit companies relied for their audience. The success of the town's theatre in drawing an audience is, therefore, a little surprising.

Perhaps it was due to the relationship between the town and its visiting companies, for it seems that the actors in Kendal were often on a close and intimate footing with the important local people who comprised their audience. In his novel, *Alwyn or the Gentleman Comedian* (1780), which he admits is based very directly on actual experience, Thomas Holcroft indicates the social importance of the actors' visits to some members of the Kendal community:

> A small assembly among the gentry and opulent tradesmen, and the players for about six or eight weeks, constitutes their highest ideals of public luxury.[29]

Alwyn himself causes a great stir, has all the young ladies of the town chasing him, and is even, "plausible enough" to gain the protection of the young gentlemen.[30] The importance of public relations with the town is emphasised when Holcroft recounts in the novel an argument between one of the company and a local squire. The quarrel resulted in the actor challenging the squire to a duel, but the rest of the company eventually persuaded the actor to withdraw the challenge. He only agreed when

> he had procured a paper, signed both by this redoubted 'Squire and his father-in-law, the purport of which was a promise not to molest the players, nor, by any means endeavour to

prevent their coming to Kendal as usual. A night or two after this affair happened the *Beaux Stratagem* was played and the audience burst into an uproar of laughter when Scrub says, "If our masters in the country receive a challenge, the first thing they do is to tell their wives", &c. and Squire Bullhead became the jest of the town.[31]

It is, of course, impossible to arrive at a detailed composition of the late Georgian audience in Kendal. Yet we can identify some individual members who are known from their diaries. One, mentioned earlier, is Benjamin Browne, the younger, Kendal's High Constable, who was of the yeoman class. On his first recorded visit to the theatre in January 1791 he paid 2s. and evidently sat in the pit (an appropriate place for that class). However, when he went in February that year and again in November 1792, he sat in the gallery (for 1s.). This may mean that the pit was crowded or that he was not suitably dressed for the more expensive seats, or simply that the usual seating "rules" were not rigidly applied in Kendal. In May 1793, Browne took his wife to a performance at a cost of 3s., which might indicate that they sat in different parts of the house: pit for her at 2s. and gallery for him at 1s. This was not an uncommon practice for husband and wife at this period.

Another member of the Kendal audience in the 1790s was the young female diarist, also mentioned earlier. She recorded five visits to the theatre in 1795. On January 3, she went with a friend, "Mrs O.", and again a week later, when she writes: "Mrs. O. popt in for tea and we strolled off to the play". On March 23, the young lady went "to the play with Anna". Her diary has an educated, sophisticated air to it, and she is obviously of upper class status. The entries are filled with accounts of visits, taking tea, playing cards, and travelling to see friends some miles from Kendal. Among her acquaintances were the Ashburners, perhaps relatives of the Thomas Ashburner who built the Market Place theatre. The young lady's social position is confirmed by the fact that in February 1795 she sat in the stage-box.

The last known member of the Kendal audience is another local diarist, called Stephen Witton, who began to record his "Remarkable Events" in 1807.[32] His erratic spelling, use of colloquial phrases, and catholic tastes in entertainment (ranging from well-known opera singers to the Hottentot Woman) suggest that he was of the lower middle class. He provides us with invaluable, personal opinions on performances in Kendal, views which probably reflect those of many of his contemporaries and which often run counter to the more bland reviews and comments in the press. The diary seems to include a reference to almost every performer in Kendal between 1807 and 1855 and he is often very scathing and dismissive in his criticism, one of his favourite derogatory terms being "a hum" (cheat or hoax). When he refers to a performance he did not see himself, he makes comments such as: "I heard no cracks of him no great thing I suppose".

In at least the first thirty years of the recorded history of Kendal theatre, there was considerable active involvement in theatrical affairs on the part of many townspeople. Men of standing and position in the town were several times concerned with the building of playhouses, and local patronage in the form of "bespeaks", while not over-liberal, did occur. The earliest recorded bespeak in

Kendal was, in fact, in 1813, when the Kendal Masons requested a performance of *West Indian*. The bill for that evening also included two masonic songs and an epilogue spoken in the character of a Mason's wife, which were presumably specially devised by the company.[33]

Some local people became even more closely involved with the theatre, to the extent of taking part in performances. In February 1807, for example, the role of Peter in *The Stranger* was played by "a Gentleman of Kendal", and so was Robin Roughead in *Fortune's Frolic* on the same bill. (Whether it was the same gentleman is not clear.)[34] The playbill for March 20 in that year includes a song performed "By a Gentleman of this town" and another "by a Gentleman of Troutbeck Bridge (his first appearance)". In addition, the cast list on the playbill for the pantomime *Cinderella* that season has a manuscript note which states that "children of the town" played Cupids.[35]

In view of this evidently close relationship between the actors and their Kendal audiences it may seem surprising that after 1817 the theatre had such a struggle to survive in the town, but this was the case. That struggle and its underlying reasons will be explored in the next "act" of the drama.

Notes
1. In the possession of the South Lakeland District Council.
2. C.N. p. 56.
3. J. Romney, *Memoirs of the Life and Works of George Romney*, 1830.
4. T. Holcroft, *The Life of Thomas Holcroft*, 1925, pp. 154-5.
5. F. C. Wemyss, *Theatrical Biography*, Glasgow, 1848.
6. W. Sayer, *History of Westmorland*, 1847, p. 124.
7. C.N., p. 156.
8. According to Parish Registers in W.R.O.
9. C.N., p. 166.
10. February 12, in the possession of the South Lakeland District Council.
11. Conveyance of December 29, 1877, in the possession of the South Lakeland District Council.
12. J.F.C., p. 344.
13. C.N., p. 156-7.
14. *Op. cit.*, p. 78.
15. In the Houghton Library, Harvard. (I am grateful to Bruce MacDonald of Northeastern University, Massachusetts for these details).
16. In the possession of Vaux Breweries, Sunderland.
17. C.N., p. 156-7.
18. J.F.C., p. 319.
19. *Memoranda* in W.R.O.
20. F. C. Wemyss, *op. cit.*, p. 35.
21. T. Wilkinson, *The Wandering Patentee*, II, York, 1975, p. 154.
22. Browne, *Memoranda, op. cit.*
23. Playbill, January 8, 1801, S.R. III.
24. J. Doran, *Annals of the English Stage*, III, 1888, p. 212.
25. K.C., February 13, 1813.
26. W. G., April 1, 1815.
27. F. C. Wemyss, *op. cit.*, p. 38.
28. F. L. Thompson, *Landed Society in the Nineteenth Century*, 1963, p. 114.
29. T. Holcroft, *Alwyn, or the Gentleman Comedian*, I, 1780, p. 31.
30. *Ibid.*, II, p. 75.
31. *Ibid.*, II, p. 8.
32. S. Witton, manuscript diary in the possession of Mr. R. G. Plint.

33. *K.C.*, May 1, 1813.
34. Playbill, February 23, 1807, in Kendal Museum.
35. Playbill, February 9, 1807, in Kendal Museum.

Act II:
"An Assemblage of all the Unregenerate": Kendal Theatre Loses Support (1818-1838)

The *Kendal Chronicle* of April 18, 1818, declared that the Theatre Royal, Kendal, was "To be Let for a Term of Years", it being "a very neat, well-finished Theatre . . . late in the possession of Mrs. Butler". On September 5, the same newspaper announced that the theatre was to be taken by Mr. Howard, "the manager of the Theatre Royal, Lancaster, whose liberality and spirited conduct have gained him so much popularity and public patronage". In 1817, Howard had taken over not only the Lancaster theatre, but also those in Preston and Blackburn, and by 1819, in addition to Kendal, his circuit included Bolton and Warrington.

His first season in Kendal, one of only six weeks, began on Easter Monday, April 18, 1819, with three special "attractions": Mr. Usher from the Royal Coburg Theatre, London; his wife, billed as being from the Covent Garden Theatre; and Mr. Holland, the famous Harlequin. Other "eminent artists" that Howard brought to Kendal were Clara Fisher and her sisters Caroline and Amelia, for three nights from April 23. Clara, aged eight, was described as a "very rare and singular specimen of prococious [sic] talent", and as "the prettiest and cleverest little woman we have seen for a long time".[1] Appropriately enough, the Fisher sisters appeared in *Lilliput* (Garrick's piece written for children), though this was followed by Clara as Richard III.

A reviewer praised Howard for being "unremitting in his efforts to produce a perpetual succession of novelty and amusement", and in his farewell address on May 22, Howard himself indicated the success of the season by saying that "the receipts have by far exceeded my most sanguine expectations". However, other press comments that summarised the season were hardly fulsome, remarking that there was "a respectable attendance" at the manager's benefit, and that the season "has not been unsuccessful".[2]

Perhaps in a further attempt to boost audiences in the next season (1820), Howard engaged "the celebrated Mr. H. Johnston", the late manager of the Drury Lane Theatre, for the opening night on April 10. Henry Johnston had, in fact, performed in Lancaster with Howard's company the previous week.[3] Kendal then welcomed back the diminutive Clara Fisher, who played, of all parts, Falstaff in *Henry IV*,[4] and she and her sisters remained with the company until the end of April.

The season ended on June 2 and the company went to perform in Lancaster during the race-week, but unusually they returned to Kendal in September of the same year, also for the (newly revived) races. Howard shows how unusual this visit was by apologising on the playbill of September 16 for taking his benefit out of the regular season but hoping "the serious loss sustained in the spring will prove excuse".[5] What this loss was is not explained.

During the next season in the spring of 1821, presumably in an attempt to flatter and attract the town audience, the company employed scenery with a local flavour (backdrops of the castle, for example). This seems to have been a feature of Howard's management for he did the same in Lancaster.[6] As in the previous year, the company re-opened the Kendal theatre for the race-week, the gross receipts for the first night being given to the race-funds.

Howard does not seem to have performed himself in Kendal during the season of 1822, though his company did. Despite the obvious advantages of the revived races the Kendal theatre that year had "thin" audiences. Theatre, it seemed, was no longer in fashion or favour. This may explain why the company did not return to Kendal in 1823, though they performed in Lancaster during both the spring and summer assizes, and were in Penrith for "a short campaign".[7] It is probable that Howard sold the lease of the Kendal theatre at the end of the 1822 season, for a number of different managers tried their hands during 1823.

On February 1, 1823, the theatre opened for the remainder of the winter season under the management of a Mr. Wilson. His company included a Mr. Copeland, who had been with Howard's troupe for several seasons and who was now "greatly improved". Despite Copeland's improvement, Mr. Wilson was evidently unsuccessful and, after a week, is referred to as the "quondam manager" and replaced by a Kendalian, Mr. Burrows.

He had a little more success, according to the reviews in the *Kendal Chronicle*. The company performed *The Foundling in the Forest* "in a very superior style", Mr. Diproses's Hamlet was "a performance of great merit", and the manager as Clodpole in *Barnaby Brittle* (Samuel Butler's old part) earned "our warmest approbation". Such praise, however, was tempered by criticism of Mr. Hunter, who was advised "not to appear again in *Baillie Nichol Jarvie* without being perfect" (in his lines).[8] Burrow's season had closed by the end of March, when a ball was held in the theatre.

Three months later he was followed by Mr. Alexander, styled the manager of the Carlisle and Dumfries theatres, who opened the Kendal theatre for a few nights in order to present "that great Luminary of the Art", William Macready.[9] The *Kendal Chronicle* reviewer commented that "for a length of time the theatricals here have been gradually declining",[10] so clearly Mr. Alexander hoped to ensure his company's success by the engagement of this star. Macready performed Macbeth and Virginius on successive nights. A long review of August 2 lavished praise on him: "of his acting it is impossible to speak too highly". But the actor gives a rather different view of the occasion when he describes in his autobiography the difficulties he encountered with the inadequate and under-rehearsed actors in Alexander's company with whom he had to perform:

> The corps dramatique arrived in the town too late for the rehearsal of *Virginius*, and I had to undergo during the first two acts a succession of annoyances in the scenic deficiencies and in the inaccuracies of the players. My unhappy temper was severely tried under the repeated mortifications I experienced, but in the third act of the play, where Siccius Dentatus should

be discovered on a bier with a company of soldiers mourning over him, I saw the old man, who represented the Roman Achilles, lying on the ground, and two men standing near. This was too absurd! the body having to be borne off in sight of the audience. I positively refused to go on. "Oh, pray, Sir", urged the manager, "go on: the men have rehearsed the scene and you will find it all right". In vain I represented that the men "could not carry off the old man". "Oh, yes, indeed, Sir", reiterated the manager, "they perfectly understand it". There was nothing for it but submission. After some delay the scene was drawn up and disclosed the three as described. On I went and uttered my lamentation over the prostrate veteran, but when I gave the order "Take up the body, bear it to the camp" – to my agony and horror the two men, stooping down, put each arm under the shoulder of the dead Dentatus, raised him upon his feet, he preserving a corpse-like rigidity, his eyes closed, and his head thrown back, and arm-in-arm the trio marched off at the opposite side of the stage amid roars of laughter from the convulsed spectators. I need not observe how difficult it was for audience or actor to recover their serenity after such a travestie.[11]

Macready's experiences are perhaps a fitting epilogue to that period of the town's theatre history. Three months afterwards the theatre was sold to the Presbyterians, who, according to Curwen

opened the theatre in the Woolpack Yard in the month of November, 1823, and worshipped there, with the gaudy scenery hanging around them.[12]

The irony of Kendal's theatre passing into the hands of the church ought not to be overlooked. The gradual decline of the theatre's popularity throughout the country in the early 1820s can in part be attributed to religious opposition. The general outbreak of moral indignation at the unsavoury nature of theatre-going was largely prompted by the contemporary religious revivals that followed the political upheavals of the first twenty years of the nineteenth century.

Theatre had, of course, received long-standing opposition from the church. The attacks were based not only on the principle of the evil of acting *per se*, but on the immoral character of actors, classed, as they had been for centuries, as vagabonds. The reputation of the early "strollers" was not good; "Take the linen from the line, the strolling players are here" is said to have been once a familiar cry.[13] Many towns refused to allow players to stay, not just to protect their underwear, but for religious reasons or simply because of a deep-rooted local prejudice. Even the more obviously respectable members of regular circuit companies of the 1800s were liable to abuse. In 1805, a company of actors was driven out of Whitehaven because a local man accused them of bringing a curse on the town, thus causing the failure of the local fishing fleet.[14] The opposition to companies in most places seems not to have been of such a superstitious nature, but nevertheless it carried the full weight of the church and rested on the position of general and moral disapproval.

The greatest religious opposition to the theatre at the beginning of the nineteenth century came from the non-conformists, in particular, the Quakers and Methodists. And Kendal, of course, had a long tradition of non-conformity, and the attitudes towards the stage prevalent among these groups were already apparent in the eighteenth century. Thomas Holcroft remarks (in 1790):

Neither are those wanting, who inveigh with warmth and acrimony against these amusements [theatre]. This is not wonderful when we recollect that great part of the inhabitants of Kendal are Quakers.[15]

The Quaker population in the town had increased by 1801 to 880 out of a total population of 7,978, which does not seem a high proportion, but during the first decades of the nineteenth century the non-conformist manufacturers, and especially the Quakers, became the main employers in Kendal. They consequently provided leadership in industrial, religious and social matters for the large numbers of craftsmen who formed the majority of the town's lower middle class. Even at a time of peak popularity for the theatre, such as 1813, gentle warnings were issued by the local press:

> While rendering the just need of praise when merit is conspicuous, we are not to allow the modesty of nature to be overstepped without notice. In giving hints of this kind (should occasion call for it) we wish to be gentle. A well-regulated theatre affords a rational source of amusements, from whence the low stuff of a Fantoccini should ever be banished, that the cheek of modesty may remain untinged with a blush.[16]

Many playbills of the time show the manager's awareness of the tightrope they walked by stressing the "moral" tendencies and intentions of a large proportion of the plays presented.

When actors took part in the music festival in 1815, not all Kendalians welcomed their stay, as Curwen points out:

> It must not be thought, however that these festivals in the Church met with unanimous approval from all, for I have before me some tracts and two bills, which were posted by John Pearson, the minister of the Inghamite Chapel [non-conformist], one on the Parish Church door and the other in Stricklandgate near the theatre.[17]

The following year the festival was held in only the theatre. Another minister, the Reverend William Whitelock of the St. George's Chapel, had also been preaching against the theatre. His campaign culminated in 1823 in the placarding of the town with a carefully designed poster. Its ingenuity warrants it full quotation:

THEATRE
"The Great and Terrible day of the Lord"
by Command of the King of Kings

at the

Theatre of the Universe
On the Eve of Time, will be performed

THE GREAT ASSIZE

or the

Day of Judgement

——

THE SCENERY

which is now actually preparing, will not
only surpass everything that has yet been
seen, but will infinitely exceed the utmost
stretch of human conception. There will be

a just Representation of All the Inhabitants
of the World, in the various and proper
Colours, and their Customs and manners will
be so exact and so minutely delineated,
that the most secret Thoughts will be discovered –

THIS THEATRE WILL BE LAID OUT AFTER A NEW PLAN

and will consist of a

PIT AND GALLERY

The Gallery is very spacious & the Pit without bottom
To prevent inconvenience there are separate doors

ACT I

Of this Grand and Solemn Piece will be opened by
AN ARCHANGEL WITH THE TRUMP OF GOD

ACT II

A PROCESSION OF SAINTS
In White with Golden harps, accompanied with
shouts of joy & songs of praise

ACT III

AN ASSEMBLAGE OF ALL THE UNREGENERATE

To conclude with an Address by

THE SON OF MAN

Tickets for the Pit are sold at every place of Temptation

Tickets for the Gallery may be had gratis at the
"Fountain opened for sin and for uncleanness"

Such was the impact of Whitelock's playbill, it seems, that the already waning theatre in the Woolpack Yard closed, and the building was sold, as we have seen to the Presbyterians.

Mr. Howard, however, was undeterred by the closure; he returned to Kendal in 1824 and opened a new "playhouse" at the Crown Inn. The first playbill of his season suggests the theatre's limitations:

> Mr. Howard respectfully announces the opening of the Theatre in the above situation which will be found fitted up in the best style the limits of the place will admit.[19]

Even so, the playbill for August 2 that year calls it the "Theatre Royal", and it had boxes as well as a pit and gallery. But this was Howard's last appearance in the town, though he did continue to manage theatres at Lancaster, Preston and Rochdale.

There is no evidence of theatrical activity in Kendal in 1825, but in 1826 two managers tried their luck. Despite the *Kendal Chronicle* claim that pieces were "got up with great care" at the "neat little theatre at the Crown Inn",[20] the season was eventually described as "one dull monotony of failure and disappointment". In the press this unsuccessful season was blamed on the excessively hot weather, but the depression in the local weaving and other trades must have played a part.

After a further year's absence, theatre returned to Kendal in 1828, and this time it was presented in yet another new playhouse – at the bottom of the Old Shambles. This area originally comprised forty butchers' shops and a public house, the Butchers' Arms, but by 1803, because of inadequate drainage, the butchers had to be moved elsewhere and their shops were converted into cottages. There are six extant playbills, dated June 11 to July 3, 1828, that announce performances at "the Theatre at the bottom of the Old Shambles". Today at the end of Old Shambles Yard is a large, empty building, which was presumably the public house that contained the theatre. The overall measurements of the building are about 21.5 metres on three floors, and the top floor once had one large room (now partitioned) about 16.5 metres in length, which would have been an acceptable size for a theatre at that time. The playbills indicate that the theatre here was far from grand, as it only had pit and gallery seats. (See Fig. 8.) No manager is named on the bills, but the leading actor, and therefore probably the manager, appears to have been a Mr. Collier. His wife and son were also in the company; a Mr. and Mrs. Collier had performed with Howard in 1822. No further information or comment is available to us on this small theatrical venture.

Then, quite unexpectedly, yet another, new purpose-built playhouse is brought to our attention. On November 2, 1828, the *Westmorland Gazette* reported: "Mr. Thomas Simpson of Watch Field, intends to erect a theatre on the old buildings adjoining the Blue Coat School". (See Fig. 9.) Simpson was a local "character", who, despite being wealthy, travelled around Kendal in an ordinary farm-cart. He was said to be the greatest racehorse breeder and race-winner the town had ever had. His interest in the races was, of course, most appropriate, since race-week was traditionally a time for theatre performances. Simpson engaged the services of a local cabinet-maker, John Richardson, as architect of the new theatre.

The building still exists and, though it is now used merely as a store, its original elegance is still apparent. It has an attractive front with a large central door approached by a flight of stone steps, flanked on either side by a window. The main entrance leads into the "upper room", which measures approximately 18.5 metres by 9.75 metres (similar measurements to those of the Richmond theatre). There are two more windows; a low one in the south wall near the south-west corner, and a second, about 3 metres up in the rear (west) wall. The room has a false ceiling, which appears to be original and which slopes from the roof height (about 9 metres) at either end towards the centre (dropping to about 6 metres). In the centre of this dipped ceiling there is an opening up to a skylight. (There is a similar sloping ceiling and rear window in the Richmond theatre.)

Fig. 8   Exterior of Old Shambles
Theatre building, 1988

Fig. 9   Exterior of New Theatre building, 1988

26

Beneath the whole of this room, at ground level, there are two "rooms" about 2 metres high, which were obviously originally built as one. They are entered by doors on either side of the front steps and could have provided space for dressing-rooms, stage machinery and traps, as suggested for the Woolpack Yard Theatre, but there is no surviving evidence for this in either the fabric of the building or the floor of the upper room. The heating in this theatre was by means of coal fires; although no fireplaces are apparent now, there is a chimney stack on the east end of the roof.

When the new theatre opened on June 22, 1829, it was described rather baldly as "a large Public room",[21] but it seems to have been a fully fitted theatre with boxes, pit and gallery, and "the Interior of the House [is] elegantly Painted and Decorated".[22] It probably held about 500 people. The opening week was said to be quite well supported and the one benefit failure of the season was attributed to the bad weather. But one reviewer in the *Kendal Chronicle* that year noted some changes:

> We blush for the departed taste and public spirit of our leading gentry. We expected to have seen a crowded house – to have seen all the talent, rank, wealth, respectability of the town present at the performance of William Tell. We expected to have seen large groups of beautiful women – mothers, daughters, wives; liberal ministers of various denominations; members of learned professions – tradesmen sitting in reverential admiration, and bestowing their assistance in heart, pocket and hand to the brilliant exertions of the performers – but alas! we were disappointed.[23]

Thomas Simpson had, in fact built this New Theatre at the period when the Quakers were at their most influential in the town. But as if the building of a theatre were not enough at such a time, shortly after, he opened the Shakespeare Inn nearby, just as the temperance movement was formed under the chairmanship of a leading Quaker, W. D. Crewdson.

Kendal's New Theatre was managed in 1829 by a Mr. Stevens, who was already the manager of the Theatre Royal, Manchester. He opened the first season with "a Powerful and Efficient Company from the principal Provincial Theatres in the Kingdom".[24] The first playbill indicates that the performers were drawn from the Theatres Royal at Sheffield, Preston, Liverpool, Dublin, York, Birmingham and Glasgow. And as this seemed to be the dawning of a new and exciting theatrical era in Kendal, Mr. Stevens gave an opening address before the first performance began.

This "new beginning" also prompted the presentation of a considerable number of plays new to Kendal, including *The Red Barn* (1828), more commonly known as *Maria Marten and the Red Barn*. This was, as the playbill announced, "founded on a late melancholy transaction, which took place at the village of Polstead, May 18, 1827". It was not however, appreciated by the reviewer for the *Kendal Chronicle*:

> We cannot but deprecate the taste which admires these Tom-fooleries in preference to the legitimate drama, and we trust that this and such like pieces will never be again performed on the Kendal boards. They are disgusting.[25]

There is no other recorded Kendal performance of *The Red Barn*. Another great nineteenth century success, however, fared better. The reviewer of *The Miller and His Men* thought the piece "better got up than we ever saw it upon a provincial stage. The Scenery and Machinery were justly admired and the acting was good".[26] Such a response led the manager to extend the season one extra night.

Two weeks after Steven's company left Kendal, the New Theatre was open again, this time under the management of a Mr. Cooper, who had had a successful season at Penrith in 1825, and, in the meantime, had acquired the Preston, Bolton, Whitehaven and Macclesfield theatres for his circuit. Despite the fact that the Kendal theatre had only been in use since June, Cooper announced that it had undergone alterations and redecoration "during the Recess".[27]

When Cooper's season closed in September he was praised for having "expended much to render the pieces so highly popular".[28] His success may have been helped by the two local charity benefits given that season: one for the Dispensary and the National School, and one for the Kendal Venison Feast (an annual event held by the gentlemen of Kendal Book Club to celebrate the glorious twelfth).

Cooper returned to the town in December to present the boy actor, Master Burke, one of many who followed in the wake of the famous Master Betty. In fact, Master Burke was considered to be a better violinist than actor. On this occasion he performed in the company of his younger brother, Master W. Burke, who also played the violin during their stay in Kendal, though it might be said he came into his own by taking the title role in *Tom Thumb*.[29]

When Cooper's company reappeared the following year they lured to Kendal a number of other well-known actors. On July 31, John Vandenhoff, considered to be "the last prominent tragedian of the Kemble school", performed King Lear, the part in which he had gained acclaim at Covent Garden in 1820. He was followed by Ellen Tree (later the wife of Charles Kean), who was engaged originally for four nights but was prevailed upon by Cooper to act one more night. Then came a face familiar to Kendal, that of Drinkwater Meadows, who had first appeared with the Butler company in 1801, and was now from Covent Garden. The next star was the "African Roscius", Ira Aldridge, who performed a number of his famous roles, such as Rolla in *Pizarro*, and stayed in Kendal for five nights. The local response to all these London performers was appreciative if not overwhelming:

> Since the commencement of the season, Mr. Cooper has, with a laudable zeal to gratify the lovers of the drama, introduced some of those ornaments who grace the provincial boards during the metropolitan recess; and if not stars of the first magnitude, yet brilliant enough to outvie the radiance of those who move in a minor sphere.[30]

Indeed, the resident actors suffered by the comparison, and Mr. Roberts was singled out for criticism because his love of "declaration" led him to neglect the playwright's intentions and leave "the audience lost in wonder at his extravagance".[32] It seems that such comparisons and criticisms had a lasting effect on public opinion. When Cooper opened the season of 1831 he indicated his intention of later having a winter season too, but on August 20 he closed "a brief and unprofitable season",[33] left Kendal and never returned. As the decline in audience numbers continued, the local press laid the blame on education and the economic depression:

> Poverty on the one hand, and the Schoolmaster on the other, have placed the people of this country in a position little calculated to foster the mimic art.

The following year (1831), the management of the theatre was taken over by Mr. Copeland, who was well known to Kendal audiences, having first performed in the town with Howard's company in 1818. It is clear that he, too, experienced difficulties in getting audiences: his playbills offer half-price seats "in order to accommodate juvenile branches of Families".[32] (Some juveniles in the town were, in fact, on strike during this period.)

The most notable theatrical event of 1832 was the engagement of the famous actor, Edmund Kean, now near the end of his career (he died in 1833). He gave one performance on March 5, when, according to the diarist, Stephen Witton, there was a very crowded house that yielded a box-office return of £42. It is perhaps a measure of the decreasing local interest in theatre that even such a "star" warranted no review in any of the Kendal newspapers.

When Copeland's company returned to Kendal for the season of 1834, the first advertisement declared that the theatre had been re-painted and that "no pains shall be spared in selecting and producing performances eminent for classic fame and modern popularity".[33] Audience opinion of the company seemed high. When Mr. Lyon performed *Richard III*, for example, he was favourably compared with Kean, and his Othello was described as a "true personation". Yet public support was apparently insufficient, for when the Copeland company left in March, the New Theatre closed its doors for ever. One of the local newspapers claimed that the building was to be converted into stables, and Curwen says it was used as a ballroom. They were both right: the upper part of the theatre did become a ballroom, and the lower part was made into two stables from which the ground remains cobbled today. A writer in the *Kendal Chronicle* castigated "the Higher Order of Society" for its neglect of the theatre and allowing it to undergo the "unhallowed alterations",[34] thus making it clear that it was the "gentry" that had deserted the theatre.

Following the closure of the New Theatre there were two more theatrical seasons in Kendal in the 1830s. After two fallow years (1835/6), a Mr. Martin and his company took up residence in the Oddfellows' Hall on Highgate in January 1837. This hall, which opened in October 1833, occupied the first floor of the building, while below it was the Nelson Tavern (now a bookshop). (See Fig. 10.) Playbills indicate that this theatre had a pit, gallery and boxes and the *Westmorland Gazette* "was much gratified in witnessing the very superior style"[35] in which it was fitted up. Whatever the style, the scale must have been less impressive since the hall is only about 11 metres long by 8 metres wide.

Martin's was the latest traditional circuit company to perform in Kendal, his circuit in 1837 including Whitehaven, Carlisle and Penrith. The first newspaper review of the company's efforts in Kendal is hardly enthusiastic, merely recommending a visit to "relieve the tedium of an idle hour".[36] Despite these rather

Fig. 10   Exterior of Oddfellows' Hall, 1988

cool comments, the company seems to have been quite successful, for their season lasted from January to July, and closed with the press comment that the actors would "long be remembered".[37] This was just as well, since their season of 1838 was not only a failure but marked the end of another era in Kendal's theatre history. For at least ten years afterwards no plays were performed in the town.

The gradual theatrical decline in Kendal between 1818 and 1838 is clearly marked in the frequent changes in management and the inexorable closure of theatres: 12 managers struggled in 5 different theatre venues during those twenty years. But in this respect Kendal was part of a national picture: it was obvious in the 1830s that the middle and upper classes no longer patronised the theatres. The reasons for this apparent withdrawal are uncertain, though a Parliamentary Select Committee of 1832 suggested that the "better class" of citizen was deterred from going to the theatre by the presence of immoral members of the community.[38] How true this was of Kendal is impossible to know, but the combination of a slump in local trade and the strong religious opposition certainly helped to extinguish interest in "straight" theatre in the town by the late 1830s.

Notes
 1. *W.G.*, April 22, 1819.
 2. *K.C.*, May 3, 1820.
 3. *Lancaster Gazette*, July 1, 1820.
 4. *W.G.*, April 15, 1820.
 5. *Lancaster Gazette*, July 1, 1820.
 6. *Ibid.*, April 7, 1820.
 7. *K.C.*, April 26, 1823.
 8. *Ibid.*, February 1 and 8, 1823.
 9. *Ibid.*, July 26, 1823.
10. *Ibid.*, August 12, 1823.
11. F. Pollock, ed., *Macready's Reminiscences and Selections from His Diaries and Letters*, 1876, pp. 215-216.
12. J.F.C., p. 322.
13. R. J. Broadbent, *Annals of the Liverpool Stage, Liverpool, 1908*, p. 32.
14. W. Donaldson, *Recollections of an Actor*, 1865, p. 92.
15. *Alwyn, or the Gentleman Comedian, op. cit.*, p. 32.
16. *K.C.*, February 20, 1813.
17. J.F.C., p. 244.
18. In W.R.O.
19. Playbill, July 30, 1824, in W.R.O.
20. August 5, 1826.
21. W. Parson & W. White, *History, Directory, and Gazetteer of the Counties of Cumberland and Westmorland*, Leeds, 1829, p. 646.
22. *K.C.*, June 20, 1829.
23. *K.C.*, July 11, 1829.
24. *K.C.*, June 20, 1829.
25. *K.C.*, July 11, 1829.
26. *Ibid.*
27. *K.C.*, August 1, 1829.
28. *K.C.*, August 8, 1829.
29. Playbill, December 19, 1829, S.R.III.
30. *W.G.*, August 21, 1830.
31. *Ibid.*
32. Playbill, November 5, 1831, in W.R.O.

33. *K.C.*, January 11, 1834.
34. *K.C.*, March 15, 1834.
35. June 16, 1837.
36. *K.C.*, May 6, 1837.
37. *Kendal Mercury*, July 1, 1837.
38. Quoted by M. Baker, *The Rise of the Victorian Actor*, 1978, p. 144.

Act III:
"Magical, Mimical, Musical and Ventriloquial New Entertainment":
Kendal's Theatrical Tastes Change (1839-1874)

Between 1839 and 1874 plays were virtually replaced in Kendal by other forms of entertainment. Theatre companies had almost ceased to visit the town, and their absence was compensated for by an increasing array of miscellaneous performers. These essentially "popular" entertainers had, of course, always appeared in the town, both alongside the "straight" actors and in close conjunction with them. The theatre programmes of the late eighteenth and early nineteenth centuries were extremely varied: not only were music and dance an integral part of many plays, but no bill would have been complete without solo songs, dances and speciality acts. And, of course, these popular entertainers continued to appear in Kendal even when an interest in and supply of drama revived in the last quarter of the nineteenth century.

We are given some fascinating insights into the popular entertainment in Kendal between 1807 and 1855 by Stephen Witton's laconic diary. It presents a lively and sometimes bizarre picture of a town full of itinerant performers of all kinds: jugglers, giants, learned pigs, educated horses, human freaks, and circuses of every size. Many performers described their shows rather vaguely as "entertainments", and these could, and often did, call upon a great variety of skills. For example, a certain Dr. Shaw's entertainment in 1859 was described as:

> his Magical, Mimical, Musical and Ventriloquial New Entertainment entitled Sketches of Ancient and Modern Times with rapid changes of Character, Costumes, Songs, Ballads and Anecdotes.[1]

Kendal's interest in such performance is, of course, typical of the contemporary national taste, a taste which in London and many large industrial towns led to the building of music-halls. Kendal did not have a custom-built music-hall, but a number of well-known artists from the "halls" did perform in the town. Among the earliest to visit was General Tom Thumb (Charles Stratton), an American midget "discovered" by Phineas Barnum, of the circus family, in 1842. For his performance in Kendal in 1846, Tom Thumb was described as being fourteen years old, twenty-five inches high and fifteen pounds in weight.

Another early music-hall star to appear in the town was Sam Cowell, famous for his cockney songs and parodies of Shakespeare. On his performance in 1859, the reviewer of the *Westmorland Gazette* remarked:

> Sam Cowell's performances though strictly belonging to the "low comedy" have nothing in the slightest degree offensive and they are irresistibly ludicrous.[2]

33

Cowell returned with his inoffensive act in 1862 and again for a "farewell" performance in 1863.

Among the stars of the 1870s to visit Kendal were the Great Vance, the famous "lion comique"; Harry Clifton, the composer and singer of "motto" songs; Maskelyne and Cooke, the illusionists and directors of Egyptian Hall, London (showplace of freaks and oddities); and Mr. and Mrs. Howard Paul, with their patriotic songs and sketches. Music Hall personalities who appeared in Kendal in the last quarter of the century included Fred Maccabe, Blondin, Lester Barrett, Sims Reeves, and, most famous of all, Albert Chevalier, "the coster's laureate".[3]

Although the swarm of "nigger minstrels" that covered the country from 1840 onwards were essentially music-hall performers, the impact they had, both nationally and in Kendal, warrants separate consideration. The first group of these "coloured" entertainers to visit Kendal was the "Ethiopian Serenaders" in 1847, but with their "little lamp black and black woolly wigs" they did not greatly impress the reviewer for the *Westmorland Gazette*:

> One of them dances in a nigger style of caper with extraordinary vigour, and uses "the bones", a kind of gigantic castanets, with great skill. The rest of the performances were comparatively nil.[4]

Later that year, in August, a second troupe called the Orleans Ethiopian Serenaders performed in the town. These were said to be a "genuine band of darkies" who had performed before the Queen, and they were expected to redeem this kind of entertainment in the eyes of Kendalians, in contrast to the previous "merest pretenders".[5] But the poor attendance suggests the town's appetite was already sated. Nevertheless, another troupe appeared in January 1848, and yet another in December 1849. Ten years or so then elapsed before minstrels again showed their black faces in Kendal and then it was a company of

> a totally different class from the ordinary troupes which swarmed throughout the country some years ago and vulgarised the negro melodies.[6]

So began a new minstrel era. Now they were usually called "Christy Minstrels" in imitation of the original American group of that name who started performing in 1843 and eventually appeared in Kendal in 1863.

The "imitators" the town saw included Butterworth's Christy Minstrels, the Matthew Brothers Monstre [sic] Troupe of Christy Minstrels and, most famous of all, the Livermore Court Minstrels, who performed in George II court costumes complete with white powdered wigs. The latter were found to be "devoid of coarseness" and "replete with humour" by the Kendal reviewer.[7]

Other musical entertainers who appeared in Kendal in this period included opera singers, though the term "opera" was used in the nineteenth century to describe a wider range of musical performances than is usual today. For example, the programme of "The Elysium Opera Troupe" who visited the town in 1864, included musical farces as well as light operettas. Opera of a more classical kind was brought to Kendal by the Grand English Opera Company who continued

34

to visit regularly in the 1870s despite difficulties created by the town's lack of a proper playhouse. (Most performances took place in the Town Hall, which only had a simple platform stage.) On one occasion, during the above company's stay in December, 1872, scenery and properties had to be borrowed from the theatre at Preston.[8]

The number of concerts during the middle years of the nineteenth century increased, though they had been a feature of Kendal entertainment for a long time. In the Victorian period, however, music was an especially significant part of everyday life and local amateur performances were as frequent as professional ones. In fact, it is often difficult at this distance to distinguish between the two. Professional concerts did clearly begin to contribute regularly to the town's social life from the 1840s. Among the performers of vocal concerts, one of the most popular in Kendal was Louisa Pyne. She gave several concerts in the 1850s, and returned again in 1872 after she had become manageress of the Royal English Opera Company at Covent Garden (as Madam Bodda Pyne).

There were occasional performances of "straight" theatre in Kendal during this period. In 1849, two companies visited the town for a season of some kind. One included Mr. and Mrs. and Master Woodford, "late of Birch's company", who had two benefits in one week. This suggests that their stay in Kendal was very short.[9] The second company that performed that year also included an actor who declared a previous connection with Birch's company. The one extant playbill, for June 23, announces that this was the first and only appearance of these "celebrated artists", though this description was probably an exaggeration. Then in 1852, two more previous members of Birch's company performed in Kendal at the Oddfellows' Hall, and in their programme of selections from *The Castle Spectre*, they were "assisted by several amateurs". (It has not been possible to trace details of Birch's company.)

It seems there were no more professional performances of plays after that until November 1854, when a company under the management of a Mr. Whyte began a "series of dramatic performances".[11] It was presumably the same company in the Oddfellows' Hall on January 17, 1855, when the benefit of Mr. Gordon, "the stage-manager of this well-conducted theatre", was announced, but no other information on this isolated season can be found.[12]

Five and a half years then elapsed before another theatre company visited Kendal. In July 1860, Joseph Holloway, the manager of the Theatre Royal, Carlisle, brought his company to the town for a seven-week season. It was very much a family affair, with Joseph Holloway, John Holloway, Mrs. Holloway and James Holloway, the "Eminent Tragedian from London". According to the bills, the latter had performed *Richard III* for 164 nights in London, including one performance before Queen Victoria, though there is no firm evidence for such a claim. This brief season gave Kendal two opportunities to see this *Richard III*.

The few available playbills advertising this company are headed "Lyceum Theatre, Kendal, Beezon Field, near the Railway station". This address suggests these performances took place in "Albert Buildings", the name given to a wool warehouse, built in the 1850s on the area known as Beezon Fields. The warehouse was conviently close to the railway line so the owner ran a track directly into the building. The bills indicate that the Holloways' "Lyceum Theatre" had a simple auditorium with prices for reserved seats at 1s., the pit at 6d., and the gallery at 3d., and at the bottom is printed "Smoking Strictly Forbidden", no doubt with the interests of the wool merchants in mind. (The building now houses the Kendal Museum.)

A further eight years passed before another company appeared in Kendal – for two nights in July (1868) at the "Shakespeare Assembly Room", an upper room in the Shakespeare Inn. Their playbill shows that the cast was dominated by the Millward family, four of them, but little else about them can be gleaned; their presence was not acknowledged by the local press and they did not re-visit the town.

About the same time, the company from the Theatre Royal, Whitehaven arrived for what seems to have been a ten-day stay. The actual year is unknown but the late 1860s or 1870 is likely; the company performed, like the Millwards, in the Shakespeare Assembly Room; their repertoire included *The Ticket-of-Leave Man*, which was first performed in 1863; the leading actor was Richard Stoddart and "Stoddart's Company" performed in Lancaster in July 1870, during which time one of the actresses died.[13] Criticism of the Kendal venue may be implied in their statement that the manager "is about to erect a Large and Commodious Wooden Building in this town, during which time he has taken the above room" (in the Shakespeare Inn).[14] This is repeated on the last extant bill for their short season but no more was heard in Kendal of them or the proposed wooden building. Apart from four performances at the "Shakespeare" during January 1870 by an unnamed company, Kendal was again deprived of "straight" theatre, until 1875, a year which marked the beginning of yet another change in theatrical fortunes.

Notes
 1. *W.G.*, December 17, 1859.
 2. July 24, 1858.
 3. *W.G.*, between May 1871 and February 1875.
 4. January 20, 1847.
 5. *W.G.*, August 14, 1847.
 6. *W.G.*, February 11, 1860.
 7. *W.G.*, January 17, 1874.
 8. *W.G.*, December 14, 1872.
 9. Playbills, January 20 & 31, 1849, in W.R.O.
10. Playbill, September 5, 1852, in W.R.O.
11. *W.G.*, November 25, 1854.
12. *W.G.*, January 13, 1855.
13. *W.G*, July 19, 1870.
14. Playbill, March 22, in W.R.O.

Act IV:
"As Performed Upwards of 200 Nights": Theatre Returns to Kendal (1875-1910)

Between 1875 and 1910 enthusiasm for the theatre grew again in Kendal. In this respect the town was in step with the rest of the country, mostly because London now imposed its theatrical tastes on the provinces in a more direct way than ever before. By the 1870s, theatre had become relatively centralised; London was the source of most entertainment, for only large provincial towns could support the traditional "stock" company, the nineteenth century equivalent of the circuit company. The growth of railway travel was a significant factor in this centralisation for it obviously made touring easier.

The first London touring company to reach Kendal (in 1875) was John Hudspeth's "Comedy Drama Bouffe and Burlesque Company" from the Globe Theatre. After performances during one week in May, such was their success that, after a night at Windermere, they returned for an additional week.[1] They gave Kendal the chance to see for the first time one of the most famous late nineteenth century melodramas, *East Lynne*. The advertisement informed the public that the play was "as performed at the Globe Theatre upwards of 200 nights".[2] (This point in theatre history marks the beginning of the "long run"; very shortly the "puffs" would talk in terms of years rather than nights.)

Eighteen months elapsed before the arrival of the next major touring show. Sarah Thorne's Comedy Company came to Kendal in June 1878, advertising the great attraction of the celebrated actor, Charles Matthews, who had made his name in the 1830s and 40s at the Olympic Theatre, London, playing in light comedies with his wife, Elizabeth Vestris. He was now seventy-five and, in fact, did not actualy perform in Kendal, owing to a "sudden indisposition". (He died a few months later.) However, his absence did not prevent the rest of the company from producing what the local press called "a most excellent entertainment".[3]

In October, 1878, R. J. Roberts, manager of the theatres in Liverpool and Blackpool brought his regional touring "Comedy, Drama and Burlesque Company" to Kendal for six nights.[4] The success of these performances enabled the company to stay another week. Their programme included four melodramas and was thus very similar to those of the London companies of the preceding years.

The next significant theatrical news was the opening of Kendal's newly built St. George's Hall, which was intended to serve as the town's theatre and was described in the local press as being "80 feet by 50 feet, with a commodious Gallery", and was capable of seating 1,200 people.[5] (See Fig. 11.) Yet, as soon as it opened, the hall came in for much criticism. Even for the first concert an extension to the stage was needed, and sightlines were found to be a problem.

However, Edward Fletcher, the new licensee of the hall brought in a major

Fig. 11 St. George's Hall in the 1880s (from A. E. Wainwright, *Kendal in the Nineteenth Century*, 1978) (by kind permission of the *Westmorland Gazette*)

touring company in September 1880, the first of a number of companies at this time to take their name from the principal play they were touring. This, the "Our Boys Company", was named after Byron's comedy, *Our Boys*, which was written in 1875 and received in Kendal its "1680th representation in the Provinces".[6]

Considerable press coverage was lavished on the leading actor of this company, Charles Dillon, who, having made his London debut at the Lyceum in 1856, was now best known as a performer of melodramas. He was, in fact, favourably compared with Charles Kean:

> The acting of the leading character was such as has probably not been witnessed in Kendal since the time when Charles Keen [sic] paid a flying visit to the town – a visit which is now only remembered by the "old stagers" of Kendal.[7]

A visit by Charles Kean is not recorded elsewhere, and it seems more likely that the reviewer intended to refer to his father, Edmund, who, of course, gave one performance in the town in 1832.

The next well-known actor to appear in Kendal (in 1883) was T. C. King, who, in 1868, had alternated Othello and Iago with Charles Dillon, and like both Matthews and Dillon was nearing the end of his career. Thus, it seems, he had to rely on his reputation to justify his performance:

> Those who remember Mr. King in his old Drury Lane days will retain impressions of his art not easily effaced.[8]

In August that year there followed an actor-manager who was very much at the beginning of his career – Frank Benson. He had appeared the previous season at the Lyceum Theatre under the watchful eye of Henry Irving, and came to Kendal with actors selected from the Lyceum company. Benson now began what was to be a long association with Kendal, and the local press showed early appreciation of his acting; the *Kendal Mercury*, for example, thought his Othello was "acted to the life".[9]

Criticism of the facilities provided by the St. George's Hall continued. A reviewer of a performance by Frank Benson in 1885 felt the play "required more ample accessories than the stage in this hall is capable of affording".[10] Yet companies continued to visit the town. The next to come was a provincial one: James Skea's "Comedy and Concert Company" who performed at St. George's Hall in November 1885. No review indicates this company's origin, but the very local nature of their tour (Milnthorpe after Kendal, for example, a town only eight miles away) suggests they were a traditional "stock" company. They were resident in Kendal for three weeks and the *Westmorland Gazette* considered the acting to be "above the average seen in small towns".[11] After a short absence in other nearby towns, the company returned in January (1886) to perform a pantomime. Their second visit of that year, however, was greeted with less enthusiasm:

> Local patrons of the drama who are not too exacting in their tastes, have little to complain of in the programmes at the Town Hall this week.[12]

(The Town Hall was increasingly being used as an alternative to St. George's

Hall.) Skea's company also brought their 1887 pantomime to Kendal, in January, while the only other theatrical event of the year appears to have been the visit of "The Original Pepper's Ghost and Spectral Opera Company" in November. This company had performed once before in the town (in 1883), when a fire on the Town Hall stage had cracked the sheet of glass that was essential to their ghost illusions.[13] On this occasion they presented selections from suitably ghostly pieces, such as *A Christmas Carol, Faust*, and *The Lancashire Witches*.

For the next four years there was another pause before the 1890s, which was characterized by the visits of an increasing number of "original" London companies bringing the latest "hits". During that decade, the audiences in the town were able to see twenty-two contemporary successes, many of which were performed by the original casts. The advertisements usually included some reference to the London theatre in which the play was first presented – "Great Gaiety Success", for example – or an indication of the length of the run or of the current tour. Almost all the shows were comedies.

Probably one of the best known of the companies was that managed by Edward Terry, a member of the "Gaiety Quartet" (with Nellie Farren, Kate Vaughan, and Edward Royce). Edward (O'Connor) Terry made his name with plays by Pinero; his production of *Sweet Lavender* ran for 684 performances at the Strand Theatre in 1888. In September 1892, Terry's company gave one performance of Pinero's *In Chancery* in Kendal.[14]

The greatest London success of this period, at least in terms of a long run, was Brandon Thomas's *Charley's Aunt*, which ran for 1,466 performances. It was presented to the Kendal public for the first time in May 1895, when W. S. Penley, the original Lord Fancourt Babberley, was still in the cast.[15] Among the five other London productions in Kendal that year was *Trilby*, the most resounding of Beerbohm Tree's successes at the Haymarket Theatre. It was performed on one night only, with Maud Jennings as Trilby and Riddell Robinson as Svengali.[16]

In 1897, the well-known touring company of Ben Greet came to Kendal for the first time. Greet had been "reared" in Sarah Thorne's stock company in Margate, and in 1886 had given the first of his many open-air productions of Shakespeare. By the time he came to Kendal, however, he was probably best known for his production of Barrett's melodrama, *The Sign of the Cross*, which the town had the chance to see during the company's visit in February and again in October 1897 when it played in St. George's Hall to "an excellent gathering".[17]

In 1898, a company was formed to run St. George's Hall, and the advertisement offering shares made proposals for its improvement:

> It is already licensed for Dramatic performances but the lack of stage convenience has practically barred Theatrical Companies from visiting Kendal. This defect the Company proposes to remedy by the provision of a Stage of ample size with an equipment equal to the requirements of all touring companies in either Comedy, Melodrama, Burlesque, Opera or Pantomime, and thus to place Kendal in the front rank as regards Theatrical Amusements. The Seating capacity will also be augmented. Electric lighting provided for the exterior of the Hall and various minor alterations affected.[18]

40

The improvements evidently had the desired effect. In the last years of the nineteenth century the number of national touring companies visiting Kendal rapidly increased, so that in both 1899 and 1901 sixteen different companies performed in the town. Lists for both years include the name of Ben Greet's Company, whose production of *The Belle of New York* (in 1901) was said to have been performed by "the largest company seen on the stage at St. George's".[19] This might indicate that the stage had, indeed, been suitably enlarged.

The increase in visiting companies continued in 1903: twenty-two offered Kendal twenty-eight difference pieces, including the famous Henry Irving favourite, *The Bells*. The now familiar mixture of London "successes" and "evergreens" appeared in 1904, with the year ending on a high note: the celebrated Mrs. Bandmann Palmer in her "419th. appearance as Hamlet".[20]

1905 and 1906 represent a peak in the number of theatre companies appearing in Kendal: there were thirty-five productions in 1905 and thirty-two in 1906, and in both years the fare included nine plays by Shakespeare. Among the favourites was *Charley's Aunt*, described in August, 1906, as "Still Running after 10 years' Absence from Kendal".[21] As if to compensate, Charley's ubiquitous Aunt paid another visit the following July, though the overall number of productions that year dropped to twelve. This total includes four Bensonian Shakespeares as a Christmas attraction.

There was no production of a play by the bard in 1908, but Kendalians could see nineteen others, including *The Sign of the Cross*, as performed by a company run by Ben Greet's daughter, Harriet. Of the seventeen productions available to the town in 1909, seven were declared to be "new" pieces from London, while one, *Dairymaids*, was declared to be "Kendal's Record Piece".[22] Judging by both the proportion of the total number of productions and accounts of audience numbers, Shakespeare was also popular in Kendal at this time. In 1896, Benson's company had audiences "Much above the average",[23] and 1910 began and ended with Shakespeare: three by the "Premier Shaksperean Company" in January and six by the faithful Bensonians in December.

However, this apparent growth in the demand for and popularity of theatre in this period was not universal in Kendal. When an interest in theatre began to revive in the 1870s, and, indeed, when Kendal audiences started to increase, religious opposition to theatre in the town had again reared its head. In 1878, the *Westmorland Gazette* reported:

> The second week of the performances of the Blackpool Prince's Theatre Company at the Kendal Town Hall has not witnessed such excessively crowded audiences as were attracted last week, but the attendance has been very fair, and the enjoyment of the visitors has been considerably enhanced by the absence of the crushing and the heat. It is a question, what it would perhaps be rather difficult to answer, whether playgoers have to thank for this increase of comfort, the fire-and-brimstone tracts, denunciatory of the stage, which have not only been circulated in the town, during Mr. R. J. Roberts' visit to Kendal, but posted up in numbers on the internal walls of certain of our factories.[24]

So while in London and other towns in the 1870s, the church and theatre were coming together to form the Church and Stage Guild, in Kendal the battle continued. It was perhaps as a result of the prevailing religious views on theatre, that the opening of Kendal's new and prestigious St. George's Hall in 1880 was celebrated by a performance of *The Messiah*.

One of the original drawbacks of this hall as a theatrical venue was that each company wishing to perform there had to obtain a special licence. Consideration of this problem was made in 1886, when

> Alderman Robinson pointed out the advantages that would be gained to the ratepayers through the hall being licensed, and stating that offers were repeatedly abandoned through the hall not being licensed for stage plays. The application was vigorously opposed by Mr. T. Crewdson Wilson, a member of the Town Council. The Bench refused the application. [25]

Suffice it to say Mr. T. Crewdson Wilson was a Quaker.

By the 1890s, however, religious sections of the community seemed to be relaxing their views, even to the extent of seeing that drama offered positive advantages, as implied in this *Westmorland Gazette* account of 1897:

> On Wednesday another of the series of entertainments arranged by the Presbyterian Young Men's Society to raise money towards the cost of the new chapel took place at the Town Hall, Mr. Graham Moffat and Miss Kate Moffat giving dramatic recitals. [26]

And so it was not religion that was to be the downfall of theatre now but the opposition from a new opponent: the cinema. As early as 1893 there were signs of things to come. In common with other towns, Kendal was offered its first taste of the exciting new medium as part of variety, music-hall style entertainment – with Poole's "Myriorama". This was a sequence of pictures shown in rapid succession to give the impression of movement.

In 1897, the "cinematographe" appeared for two weeks at St. George's Hall, showing "film" of the Queen's Diamond Jubilee Procession. Other examples of early cinema experiments occurred in Kendal in the first few years of this century – such as the "bio-scope" and the "phono-cinema" – but their effect was held at bay by the touring theatre companies from London. Then, in 1908, the first kind of "animated pictures" appeared in the town and quite suddenly, it seems, theatre was under threat from this new quarter. In 1910, at the St. George's Hall Kendalians were able to see forty-two nights of live theatre and forty-eight nights of Atroy's Animated Pictures. Another battle was on.

Notes
1. *W.G.*, May 29, 1875.
2. *W.G.*, May 15, 1875.
3. *W.G.*, June 22, 1878.
4. *W.G.*, October 5, 1878.
5. *W.G.*, July 2, 1881.
6. *W.G.*, September 18, 1880.
7. *W.G.*, September 25, 1880.
8. *W.G.*, June 23, 1883.
9. August 25, 1883.
10. *W.G.*, September 12, 1885.
11. *W.G*, December 12, 1885.
12. *W.G.*, November 6, 1886.

13. *W.G.*, June 2, 1883.
14. *W.G.*, September 3, 1892.
15. *W.G.*, May 11, 1895.
16. *W.G.*, August 15, 1896.
17. *W.G.*, October 16.
18. *W.G.*, August 17.
19. *W.G.*, January 25.
20. *W.G.*, December 31.
21. *W.G.*, August 4.
22. *W.G.*, November 13.
23. *W.G.*, April 11.
24. October 19.
25. *W.G.*, February 27.
26. January 23.

Act V:
"A Play not a Picture":
Kendal Theatre competes with the Cinema
(1911-1965)

1911 saw the real beginning of the dominance of the cinema in Kendal entertainment; for a total of thirty-two weeks pictures were on show. Live performances were now seriously curtailed. During that year, one local stock company (Inée Howard's) made four visits; a revue-style show, *The Arcadians*, appeared in March; three performances of *Niobe* were brought "at great expense" from the Kennington Theatre, London; and there were three nights of a new musical play, *Lady Lavender*, on tour from the Theatre Royal, Manchester. The last live event of the year was a "Dramatic Recital of Shakespeare's Heroines" by the great actress, Ellen Terry.[1] But that was all; a sudden reduction in live entertainment from the preceding few years.

The pattern continued in 1912. Such was the importance of the animated pictures that St. George's Hall appears as the "St. George's (Picture) Hall" in the May *Westmorland Gazette*. There were only thirty nights of live performances that year, including three separate visits by Inée Howard's company and three nights of Shakespeare from Benson and company.

The inexorable growth of the film as entertainment is reflected in the 1913 *Westmorland Gazette* "Public Notices" page. The issue of January 18 announces the opening of "The Picture House": the management of St. George's Hall had "transformed the lower hall into a handsome and up-to-date picture theatre". This had seats for 650 and a 14' screen. On July 3, 1913, the town's second cinema – Kendal Kinema – opened in Sandes Avenue. Yet, despite this seemingly overwhelming opposition, eleven theatre companies played for two or three nights each during the course of the year. Most notably among these was Kendal's first opportunity to see "the record-breaking Lancashire play", *Hindle Wakes*, which had been nurtured by Annie Horniman, founder of England's first repertory theatre in Manchester.[2] In contrast, the last theatrical event of 1913 in Kendal invited the locals to see "the real TANGO dance" in the *Lady Slavey*.[3]

The first few months of 1914 provided the town with two London shows: *Eliza Comes to Stay* from the Criterion Theatre and *The Glad Eye*, which the publicity declared had been "fifteen months the rage of London".[4] The new 'sub-title' given to the St. George's Hall in March – "The Central Cinema and Varieties" – now indicated the local and national trend for presenting variety programmes that in addition to the usual dancers, singers, jugglers and comedians, included a section of films. Six such programmes appeared in Kendal between March and December 1914. More traditional theatre fare was limited to two nights of *'Neath the Lion's Paw*, two of *Gypsy Love*, three of *The Girl in the Train*, and two of the old favourite, *Charley's Aunt*.

Films continued to dominate public entertainment in Kendal (as elsewhere) during the First World War, while "live" shows tried to compete by becoming increasingly "light" and mixed in form and title: musical revues, musical comedy revues, musical burlesques. After the war the cinema still played an important part in Kendal's social life, though in the four years between 1919 and 1922 sixteen comedies and musical comedies were presented by touring companies. At the end of 1922, the Bensonian's under the direction of Lady Benson (her husband had been knighted), presented seven Shakespeare plays. Sir Frank Benson made a personal visit the following year and the number of other touring theatre companies increased to fourteen, despite St. George's Hall now being styled the "Leading Picture Hall in the County". (See Fig. 12.)

Fig. 12   St. George's Hall as a cinema in the 1920s
(kindly given by Mr. P. Duff)

This slight halt in the theatrical decline lasted into 1924, when nine companies came to Kendal to compete with the pictures, five of them claiming some kind of "direct descendancy" from London theatres. In addition, Benson brought the annual supply of Shakespeare. Even more significantly, 1925 opened with the unusual offering at St. George's Hall of two continuous weeks by one company: Hamilton Deane's Repertoire Company, who presented eleven productions, including a version of *Dracula* written by Deane himself (in collaboration with John Balderston).[5] These two weeks were followed by a week of pantomime before the hall again became a cinema. Films were interrupted later in the year by three touring companies making brief visits and the faithful Bensonians playing for a week.

Hamilton Deane's Company were in Kendal for another two weeks at the beginning of 1926 (with eleven productions that still included *Dracula*), and after that the town had the chance to see the most successful musical of 1925, *No, No, Nanette*. Three familiar musical comedies appeared between films in February and March; then when a touring London production of *The Sport of Kings* was advertised for three nights at the end of July, the management felt compelled to draw the public's attention to the fact that this was "a very fine Theatrical Company and not a Picture".[6] Four musical/comic successes, not previously seen in Kendal, were performed in August, September and November, and the Bensonians paid their regular visit with a repertoire of six plays, also in November. On this occasion Sir Frank had the misfortune to fall down the stairs of a Kendal hotel, had twenty-three stitches in a head wound, and was prevented from performing.[7] However, the year ended on a happier note with another opportunity for Kendalians to see *No, No, Nanette*.

The next year (1927), like the previous two, opened with two weeks of repertoire by Hamilton Deane and Company (and a third showing for *Dracula*). Between the usual subsequent films there were six musical comedies (mostly three nights each) and one week of Bensonian Shakespeare. This time Sir Frank survived the pitfalls of his hotel to give a lecture on *Henry V* and perform "the interesting feat of walking from Carlisle to Kendal".[8] Unlike his nineteenth century counterparts the actor performed this for the sake of exercise and not from necessity.

Hamilton Deane's two weeks of repertoire in 1928 were said to come "direct from London Theatre Season", and, in addition to the inevitable *Dracula*, the programme now included a version of *Frankenstein*. Then after three nights of the musical comedy, *Yvonne*, at the end of January, the film schedule resumed. This was, however, interrupted in April by Bannister Howard's Company with three performances of the (aptly named) *Cuckoo in the Nest*. When the same company returned in September with the Ben Travers farce, *Rookery Nook*, the advertisement declared in bold lettering that it was "A PLAY – NOT A PICTURE".[9]

In 1929, the Hamilton Deane Company run was reduced to six nights – and *Dracula* was excluded. Apart from a few performances of *Rose Marie*, two Arnold Ridley plays (*The Ghost Train* and *Wreckers*) and another Travers farce, *Plunder*, films were shown for the rest of the year. And the opening of the new decade saw the continuation of this theatrical decline. Hamilton Deane and Company appeared for six nights (with *Frankenstein* but not *Dracula*) in their traditional January slot, after which a production of Cinderella ran for a week. But in April "talkies" hit Kendal and films took over again.

This trend was reinforced in 1931 by the opening of Kendal's third cinema,

46

the Palladium, also in Sandes Avenue, where it remains today. The only theatrical performances that year were six nights of *Dick Whittington* in January and seven nights by Deane's company in December. No live theatre was presented in Kendal in 1932 and that of 1933 was limited to one week by a company appearing in the Town Hall with six plays, four of which were Shakespeare. Between 1934 and 1937 the only live entertainment was single weeks of variety shows; there was no theatre at all in 1938, and 1939 had one week of pantomime.

The only – but interesting – professional theatre event of 1940 in Kendal was the visit of the Old Vic Theatre Company, who moved out of war-time London and made their headquarters at the Victoria Theatre, Burnley, from which they toured the north. The Old Vic was the first company to appear under the auspices of CEMA (the Council for the Encouragement of Music and the Arts), which was founded in January 1940 specifically to enable art to go to culturally deprived areas. In Kendal in October the company gave one performance of *The World is Yours* and one of *She Stoops to Conquer*. The cast was headed by Esmé Church, who also produced, Alec Clunes, Sonia Dresdel, and Renee Asherson, and "cleverly contrived screens and draperies supplied the effective scenery".[10]

The Old Vic also gave Kendal its only live theatre of 1941, returning with *Trilby, Twelfth Night*, and *She Stoops to Conquer* for one week in January; with *Thunder Rok*, produced by Tyrone Guthrie, for one week in June; and with three nights of *The Merchant of Venice* in November.[11] Unfortunately for the north, the Old Vic Company returned to London in 1942 and for the next three years films were the only form of dramatic entertainment in Kendal. Then in the June of 1945 the town was again host to the Old Vic Company, this time for three nights of their production of Shaw's *Arms and the Man*, which had opened in Manchester and featured Laurence Olivier as Sergius. Sadly there are no local reviews of these performances.

But placed unobtrusively on the *Westmorland Gazette* Entertainments page in August of that same year was an advertisement for "The Theatre Westmorland is Waiting For". This declared that Theatre Workshop, under its producer Joan Littlewood, would open in "Kendal High School Theatre" (Longlands Girl's School) with productions of Molière's *The Flying Doctor* and a new ballad-opera, *Johnny Noble*.[12] The subsequent review of the week's performances was headlined "Venture Starts Well in Kendal" and described the Molière as "brilliantly produced". The reviewer went on to quote the programme note: "The Scheme is an ambitious one but we feel sure that the people of Westmorland will support it" and, added the reviewer, "They should".[13]

The reason that Theatre Workshop (later to take over London's Stratford East Theatre) opened in Kendal is explained by one of the actors, Howard Goorney:

> A building in which to rehearse and play had been offered to us by John Trevelyan, Director of Education for Westmorland and a friend of Joan's. It was in Kendal and had been requisitioned during the war, but when the time came it was still not available. Nevertheless, we decided Kendal would be a quiet, pleasant place in which to experience our birth pangs. So we rented the large top floor of the Conservative Party Headquarters, and during June we moved there from Manchester.[14]

After a week's performances in Kendal the company toured the immediate region, returning in October to present *Don Perlimplin* and *Belisa* (by Lorca) and a "new production" of *Johnny Noble* at St. George's Hall. No review was offered this time by the *Westmorland Gazette*, but Howard Goorney perhaps reveals why:

> *Don Perlimplin* . . . at once became a *cause célèbre*, dividing the theatre-goers of the town. Some were so disgusted they crossed the street to avoid me – I was playing Don Perlimplin. Others came up to congratulate me. Today, even Mary Whitehouse would let it go without comment, but I suppose it's not surprising that in that time and place some people were disturbed by an old man's obsession for a woman young enough to be his daughter and lines like "Between my thighs the sun swims like a fish", sung by a beautiful Swedish actress Kristin Lind.[15]

The company performed a third and last time in Kendal in the summer of 1946. Their three night programme now included a new anti-Atom bomb play, *Uranium 235*, but that, the only live theatre of the year, passed without local comment. Later that summer Theatre Workshop moved to a new base in Middlesbrough.

The only three nights of live theatre of 1947 were supplied by the Southport Repertory Company with *Jane Eyre*, while the three Kendal cinemas were in continuous action. This company returned with three nights of *The Shop at Sly Corner* in March, 1948, and three of *An Inspector Calls* in October of the same year. 1948 also saw a visit by the Young Vic Theatre Company in Dekker's *The Shoemaker's Holiday* (in April); then a production of *Lilac Time*, for which the advertisement was again mindful of the competition by stressing that this was "Not a Film, but a "Live" Show, Actual Professional London Company with Special Orchestra".[16] Kendal ended that year with a traditional pantomime, *Cinderella*, starring Wee Georgie Wood, and 1949 opened with another – *Robinson Crusoe* – which came to the town *via* Preston and Salford.

But August 1949 marked a significant change in the fortunes of Kendal's live theatre. The August 6th issue of the *Westmorland Gazette*, under the headline "Kendal Mayor Welcomes Repertory Players", announced the arrival of the Frank Fortescue Players with a season of weekly repertory (in the St. Georges Theatre). (Fig. 13.) The Mayor is quoted as saying that "the company were filling a need in the town" and expressing the hope that "the public would support the new venture". Frank Fortescue was one of the two impressarios of the 1940s, who dominated the repertory touring field, the other being Harry Hanson. In 1949, Fortescue had companies in Birmingham, Chesterfield, Cleethorpes, Dunfermline, Inverness, Kirkcaldy, Manchester, St. Helen's, Southend-on-Sea, Wigan and Wakefield – and Kendal.

The tradition of weekly "rep" – with its demanding grind for the actors who rehearsed one play in the day and performed another at night each week – lasted until the early 1960s. The playwright, John Osborne, joined one of Harry Hanson's companies as an actor in the early 1950s and gives us his view of the experience:

> Hanson's companies were dreaded as the last funk-hole for any actor, but they were not so easy to penetrate. If there was a Hanson kind of theatre, there was a Hanson kind of actor, defeated from the outset and grateful to have any sort of job at all. They were apologetic

48

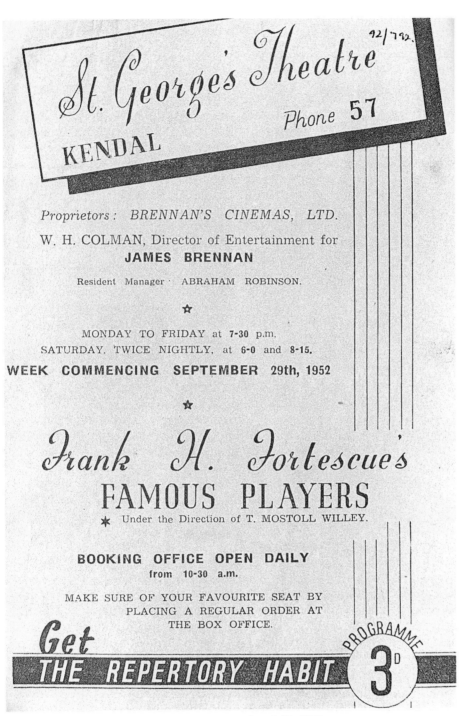

Fig. 13   Fortescue handbill, 1952

about themselves, if not among themselves. Equity representatives were unknown to speak, fluffs and dries were entered into a book by the stage director and other misdemeanours, if committed enough times, ensured the sack, administered literally according to the Hanson Book. He was the theatre's Gradgrind and his theatres were administered like workhouses of despair . . .[17]

Unfortunately, there are no Kendal reviews of the Fortescue Players, who performed almost continuously in the town between August 1949 and July 1953, though the similarity of the repertoire of Osborne's Hanson company – "pre-20s melodrama . . . hack adaptations of *Dr. Jekyll and Mr. Hyde, Gaslight, Dracula, Frankenstein, Charley's Aunt*, and low, forgotten farces"[18] – and that of the Fortescue Company in Kendal may lead one to expect the standard of performances also to be similar. Yet it would seem that Kendalians did actually "Get the Repertory Habit", as the weekly advertisement in the *Westmorland Gazette* urged; the company played six nights a week, twice on Saturdays.

In the first year the repertoire was predominantly light and comic, spiced with the odd classic, a version of *Wuthering Heights*, for example, though two of the productions were described as being unsuitable for children. An additional, and probably significant, attraction was the provision of a licensed bar for patrons.[19] The programme for 1950 showed a shift towards old favourites – *Rookery Nook, East Lynne, Gaslight, See How they Run, Sweeney Todd*, for example, – and those that catered for regional tastes – four Lancashire comedies, including *Hindle Wakes*. This latter trend was even more apparent in 1951, which began with a "Premiere" of Walter Greenwood's *Too Clever for Love*, and then the company went on to present seven other Lancashire comedies, one of which – *Bed of Roses* – was given the distinction of a two-week run.

The advertisment for February 3 (1951) announced that the company had "an Entirely New Cast of Players"[20] – an important consideration for an audience that might have become bored with seeing the same actors each week. The repertoire, however, looked more familiar: it included *Dracula, Charley's Aunt, Trilby, Jane Eyre*, and *Lady Windermere's Fan*. Two new and intriguing additions to the list, however, were *Stop It Ada* and *He Came To Stay*, written by "Archie Douglas of Kendal".[21]

Three pantomime-style shows – *Little Bo-Peep, Cinderella*, and *Red Riding Hood* – carried the Fortescue Players into 1952. They then performed Tennessee Williams' *A Streetcar Named Desire*, which, it was claimed, gave "full rein to the acting abilities of the cast".[22] Whether this went to the actors' heads we do not know, but the following week (beginning January 19) the company adopted a new title: Fortescue's "New West End Repertory Company". This change brought about productions of comedies (mostly now forgotten), six of which were described as being "from different London theatres" and two were "prior" to London runs. But for reasons unstated performances stopped in Kendal at the end of September, when St. George's Hall changed back to showing films. We can only presume that once again theatre audiences were dwindling.

The company returned in 1953, but not until the middle of February and without "West End" in their title. The repertoire was again mostly comic and

50

familiar, including two pieces by Ivor Novello and one by Noel Coward. One new and topical piece, however, was presented in April – *To See The Queen* – sub-titled "a Coronation Comedy".[23] The following month the company was described in the press as the "NEW Repertory Players under the direction of Kenneth Laird".[24] But this "new" company was shortlived; they only performed in Kendal for a further nine weeks. On July 16, after the last performance of a piece ironically called *Glad Tidings*, St. George's Hall ceased to be a theatre and once again became a cinema. We can assume that, in common with other theatres in the country, Kendal's was feeling the effect of yet another new entertainment medium, television. However, the dominance of the film in the town's public leisure activity reasserted itself in the second half of the 1950s and early 1960s. Between 1954 and 1960 live professional theatre in the town was limited almost entirely to an annual commercial pantomime, presented by Jack Gillam Entertainments, and featuring a series of "north country comedians", made famous of course, by radio and television. The *Westmorland Gazette* failed to offer any comments on these or, indeed, on two shows presented in 1958 that one might have expected to have stirred up the more conventional Kendalians: "a Sensational New Revue: *Strip-Tease Peep Show*", and *A Girl Called Sadie*, described as "a sordid study of a family where sex, greed, murder and squalor walk hand in hand".[25] These indicate very clearly the parlous state of provincial theatre, not only in Kendal, but throughout most of the country at this time.

Then in January 1959 a commercial management (that of David Kirk) presented to Kendal "the most talked of play today": John Osborne's *Look Back in Anger*. The *Westmorland Gazette* preview carefully prepared its readers: "if some members of next week's audience are shocked, they cannot fail to be gripped". The additional lure for a cinema-orientated audience was the statement that the play was "shortly to be filmed, Kendal is fortunate to have the chance of seeing the play first".[26] What Kendal made of the play cannot be gleaned.

The only live professional theatre in the years 1960-65 was one week of performances in July 1960 of *Roar Like a Dove* in the "Actual London Setting", and one week, in September 1961, of a new Lancashire comedy, written by and starring the comedian Ken Platt. Then in December 1963, under the headline, "Council's Concern Over Theatre", the *Westmorland Gazette* gave an account of the town council's discussion of the "possibility of the disappearance of Kendal's only theatre". There was a plan to demolish St. George's Hall to make room for shops and offices but this was not passed because the hall was seen as being an important "social centre", (if not a theatre).[27] Then, in May 1965, St. George's became the home of bingo. So, theatre had given way to cinema; film was ousted by bingo. The pattern was a familiar, national one.

Notes
1. *W.G.*, September 16, 1911.
2. *W.G.*, September 6, 1913.
3. *W.G.*, December 27, 1913.
4. *W.G.*, February 21.

5. *W.G.*, February 25.
6. *W.G.*, July 24.
7. J. C. Trewin, *Benson and the Bensonians*, 1960, p. 250.
8. *W.G.*, November 3, 1927.
9. *W.G.*, September 29.
10. Harcourt Williams, *The Old Vic Saga*, p. 170.
11. *W.G.*, June 21.
12. *Ibid*.
13. *W.G.*, August 18, 1945.
14. Howard Goorney, *The Theatre Workshop Story*, 1981, p. 40.
15. *Ibid.*, p. 49.
16. *W.G.*, June 2, 1948.
17. John Osborne, *A Better Class of Person, An Autobiography 1929-56*, 1982, p. 246.
18. *Ibid*.
19. All repertoire details from *W.G.*
20. *W.G.*, 1951.
21. *W.G.*, July 14 & October 6, 1951.
22. *W.G.*, January 12, 1952.
23. *W.G.*, April 4, 1953.
24. *W.G.*, May 9, 1953.
25. *W.G.*, May 23 & October.
26. *W.G.*, January 9.
27. December 6.

Epilogue:
"Hoping to Satisfy all Tastes":
Kendal's Brewery Arts Centre 1969-1985

For most of this history of theatre in Kendal the focus has been on the professionals. This last phase marks, even celebrates, the integration of amateur and professional activity in the town. The growth of amateur theatre is noticeable from the late nineteenth century, but it takes on a particular importance when professional theatre in Kendal is overwhelmed by the arrival of the cinema. In the 1930s, the Kendal Amateur Dramatic Society and the Kendal Amateur Operatic Society flourished. The *Westmorland Gazette* of February 10, 1934, contains a long article on the Operatic Society's production of *Rose Marie* and wonders whether it will break box-office records. Again in the 1960s, when the combined forces of films and bingo squeezed out visiting theatre companies, the chief performances of 1963 and 1964 were two pantomimes by the Kendal Catholic Players – the church was now stepping into the breach!

Then in 1969, the plans for a Festival Theatre at Bowness, drawn up by the Lake District Theatre Trust (inspired and led by Peter Scott, then Chairman of the Provincial Insurance Company) received such opposition that it was decided to re-focus attention – on an old brewery in Kendal. The Whitwell Mark Brewery was established in 1757 (built on the site of the town house of the Quaker family, the Wilsons of Milnthorpe) and continued to brew beer until 1968. The brewery was bought for conversion into an "arts centre" in 1970 by the Lake District Trust at a cost of £23,000. The Scott Charitable Trust gave half the first phase conversion costs (£100,000); other grants were made by the Provincial Insurance Company, Kendal Corporation, Westmorland County Council, the Northern Arts Association, and the Gulbenkian Foundation.

In March 1971, Robert Atkins was appointed to be the first director of the Brewery Arts Centre. Appropriately enough, his experience included working with Joan Littlewood's Theatre Workshop. In an interview with the *Yorkshire Post* in 1972, Atkins expressed the hope that the Brewery would "satisfy all tastes".[1] The management committee's general policy document made the purpose of the whole project clear:

> The formal provision for cultural activities and entertainment locally is at a low level largely due to to the relatively small size of the community. On the other hand there is a strong tradition of self-help in the area and societies and activities of all sorts flourish . . . Our aim is to provide a home and facilities for these societies and activities . . . Our second aim is to provide a service for schools, colleges, and other educational establishments in the area . . . We intend ourselves to provide a range of activities, entertainments, and facilities aimed at drawing a wide range of members of the community to active participation in the life of the centre.[2]

The early plans for the centre included: a theatre studio, a fine arts workshop, a cinema (seating not less than 120), an arts lab/discotheque, an exhibition room, a graphic design section, social/catering area, three club rooms, offices/stores/ general workshop (plus the "usual services"). There was even discussion in the local press of the idea that the centre would "stage television programmes" and a statement that negotiations had begun with regional television companies.[3] Not surprisingly, no more was heard of this rather unrealistic scheme. The plan for a separate cinema was also dropped (despite an initial agreement by the British Film Institute to put up £25,000).

Fig. 14   Brewery Arts Centre, 1988

The Arts Centre opened its doors in 1972. (See Fig. 14.) So, two hundred and fourteen years after Kendal's first recorded playhouse opened in a converted weigh-loft, its latest occupied an old brewery. It has to be admitted, however, that the theatre facilities are far from lavish. The theatre, housed in the courtyard wing of the complex, has a fixed-seating auditorium (capacity of 150), and a plain "platform" stage 6.5 metres square, with no wing space at all. There is one entrance from backstage from the large dressing-room, up a small flight of steps. (The theatre has recently been extensively refurbished, including new seating and technical equipment.) The first performance in the theatre was by the Westmorland Youth Theatre in *O What a Lovely War!* (a piece created and first performed by Joan Littlewood's Theatre Workshop).

54

Early criticism of the Brewery centred on the suggestion that the focus was on entertainment, and a style of entertainment that mainly aimed at younger people. To overcome this a series of drama and poetry workshops was started in November 1972; as the *Lancashire Evening Post* put it:

> The workshops should to some extent counteract the criticism that has been made that the Brewery has been concentrating over-much on the provision of entertainment, mostly for the young.[4]

The theatre, it was claimed, was "a vital link with local people, for the theatre not only houses its own dramatic group, the Brewery Players, but it is used by other local groups and small touring professional companies".[5] But the small seating capacity of the theatre meant that, even if full houses were achieved, the Brewery at best could only break even financially. It was, therefore, decided to use the theatre as a cinema on a few evenings each week – once again theatre, in a sense, was being pushed out by film.

The estimated running costs for the whole centre in 1974 were £40,300 and at that time it was said to be "in the red" to the tune of £12,850.[6] A survey conducted by Lancaster University revealed that an average of 3,000 people visited the centre each week. Of those, however, only 134 went to the theatre (less than the equivalent of one full audience). This is partly explained by a second survey that showed that 46.9% of the adult sample had visited the Brewery, whereas 75% of the "under eighteen" sample had been to the centre.[7] And theatre audiences are usually drawn from those over 21. This pattern of visits became increasingly marked. In 1975, in fact, the Brewery Arts Centre Youth Committee decided to ban those under eighteen from the centre unless they were attending a function specifically organised for them; they had tended to "roam about the building and frequently make a nuisance of themselves".[8]

But there were still problems. The theatre came in for a considerable amount of local criticism when a New Year's Eve performance of *A Christmas Day at the Workhouse* was stopped by protesting members of the audience. Under the headline "Obscene Show is Halted at the Brewery" the *Westmorland Gazette* reported:

> The promised evening of "good, bawdy humour" turned to a shambles as a section of the audience reacted strongly to prostitutes reciting their case histories, mothers with venereal-diseased lips; and a man with a phallus strapped to his head . . . The play was stopped while the actors, members of the Incubus Theatre Company from London, appealed for audience cooperation. But fifteen minutes later they stopped again, and the theatre company director, Mr. Paddy Fletcher, announced: "We were warned that if we don't stop now there will be a punch-up, so that is it".

The newspaper is said to have received "a flood of complaints", but a spokesman for the theatre company said:

> I can only think of a small part of the play which could be regarded as obscene. The language was very mild. We have received no complaints at all in London.[9]

Clearly the Kendal of 1976 was not prepared to receive what London had already seen.

In June that year the town's first Festival of the Arts was held at the Brewery, but the attendance figures were again disappointing:

> People in Kendal seem to be staying away from the first ever Festival of the Arts at the Brewery. Local playwright, David Pownall's *Music to Murder By* attracted only forty people to the theatre.[10]

1976 was, indeed, a bad year for the Brewery.

In 1976, Anne Pierson took over as Director of the Arts Centre. She had had experience in both arts education and in professional theatre and under her firm guidance the integration of amateur and professional activities properly began. Anne Pierson had been responsible for founding Pocket Theatre Company, a professional touring company, and in November 1978 they made their base at the Brewery. In addition to performing at the Arts Centre, Pocket Theatre now makes extensive tours of the region and has established a very good reputation for high quality theatre. For example, when reviewing their production of Stephen Jeffreys' *The Vigilante Trail* (written specially for the company), in 1980, Robin Thornber of *The Guardian* said the piece was "performed with polished intensity by this meticulous little company".[11] The company receives subsidy from Northern Arts.

But progress at the Brewery has continued to be uneven. An article in *The Lancashire Evening Post* in 1981 declared:

> After eight years, the centre had not been wholeheartedly accepted by the community – undoubtedly because of its adventurous approach.[12]

The same article quoted Ernest Beeston, the administrator of the Scott Charitable Trusts (still a major source of finance for the Brewery), who expressed the opinion that the Brewery's reputation was higher nationally than it was locally. However, when in 1983, Pocket Theatre Company was threatened with a total cut in their grant from Northern Arts, a sustained local campaign and a petition of 1,000 signatures helped to save them. But in June, 1985, the *Westmorland Gazette* announced: "Axe is poised yet again over Pocket Theatre".[13] But in November the company was once more reprieved, by a grant of £50,000 from the Arts Association.

Current funding for the whole centre is provided by the Scott Trust (£60,000) and by the regional arts association, Northern Arts (£90,000); and in 1986 South Lakeland District Council granted £11,000, Cumbria £10,000 and Kendal Town Council £4,000. This support is indicative of the importance of the Brewery Arts Centre, not just to the inhabitants of Kendal and the surrounding regions, but, of course, to the attraction and entertainment of Lake District tourists.

But audiences for professional theatre in Kendal remain small; so the Director's policy is to bring to the Brewery the "better known" touring companies and those presenting the classics, and to limit performances to the more "popular" nights at the end of the week.[14] It is, of course, unusual for a town the size of Kendal (22,000) to have a professional theatre at all today. Equally, the Brewery is unusual and special for its wide-ranging and integrated programme of activities. The "adventurous approach" has, indeed, been marked: the Brewery organised the first International Mime Festival to be held in the north (and has now seen its third); there has been a highly successful "artists-in-residence" scheme at the centre since 1979, with mime specialists and playwrights working with professionals and amateurs; and currently the Brewery is collaborating with the YHA on a new hostel scheme, which will provide accommodation for young people working on arts courses. The achievements at the Brewery Arts Centre have been enormous; it is to be hoped that, after four hundred years of artistic struggles in the town, Kendal will now begin to appreciate its good fortune.

Notes
 1. March 30.
 2. General Policy Document, 1971, in Kendal Public Library.
 3. *W.G.*, June 25, 1976.
 4. November 21, 1972.
 5. *W.G.*, May 10, 1974.
 6. *W.G.*, December 6, 1974.
 7. *Ibid.*
 8. *W.G.*, December 12, 1975.
 9. January 9, 1976.
10. *W.G.*, June 25, 1976.
11. *The Guardian*, January 19, 1980.
12. January 8.
13. June 7.
14. Interview with Anne Pierson, February 25, 1986.